THE BOOK OF BEGINNINGS

A PRACTICAL GUIDE TO UNDERSTAND AND TEACH GENESIS

VOLUME ONE:
CREATION, FALL, AND THE FIRST AGE

HENRY M. MORRIS III

THE BOOK OF BEGINNINGS

A Practical Guide To Understand and Teach Genesis

VOLUME ONE:
CREATION, FALL, AND THE FIRST AGE

HENRY M. MORRIS III

INSTITUTE
for CREATION
RESEARCH

Dallas, Texas
www.icr.org

THE BOOK OF BEGINNINGS
A Practical Guide to Understand and Teach Genesis
by Henry M. Morris III, D.Min.

All Scripture quotations are from the New King James Version.

ISBN: 978-1-935587-09-5
Library of Congress Catalog Number: 2012930718

Please visit our website for other books and resources: www.icr.org

Printed in the United States of America.

TABLE OF CONTENTS

PREFACE

Commentaries on Genesis today range from the fanciful to the technical. The book of beginnings has been debated for centuries by theologians, linguists, and scientists. I have shelves of such commentaries in my library—and have even read most of them. My own earthly father wrote the comprehensive commentary, *The Genesis Record,* over 30 years ago. It is still in print, still used and read by many. I refer to it constantly.

Why should you take the trouble to read another book on Genesis?

Perhaps the best reason is *urgency*. If you picked up this book and are reading this little preface, you are likely to have been prompted by an uneasy sense that a lot is not going well in our government, our society, or our churches. Over the past four generations, Christianity has precipitated from a large majority belief system among those who came of age during the first half of the 20th century to something less than 15 percent of young adults entering educational institutions and the workforce today.

It is not that the fabric of our world has lost a Christian worldview; rather, there is either *no* worldview or a practical indifference toward the profound impact that is made by personal belief systems. The narrow focus on self that engulfs the thinking of many has produced a wild abandonment of moral values, plunging our world into disorder, dissipation, and despair. If you are considering this book, you are probably bothered by these conditions and are looking for ways to help those in your sphere of influence find their way out of the morass.

This book addresses the *cause* of those problems, not merely the symptoms.

Another reason is *evidence*. This is a magnificent time to examine the accuracy of the Genesis record. Displays of the design and omniscience of the Creator are more open and obvious today than ever before. Although this book is not a book on science, *information* about the discoveries of science is absolutely stunning! *Science* does not support evolution—no matter how passionately the *scientists* and educators insist on it. Surely if the God of Genesis is real, then the evidence of His creation should be readily available for all to see.

This book provides clear evidence of God's "speech" and "knowledge" presented by science.

Perhaps a final reason would be *revelation*. Origins matter. Who and what you are is important! More significantly, how you see yourself *really* matters. If humanity is nothing more than the product of random forces, then *what* I do is irrelevant—except as it satisfies my own wishes. If I am nothing more than a "higher order" of grunting anthropoid, then I can grunt and throw my weight around just like they do. If, however, I am the unique creation of an omnipotent and omniscient God who loves me and has a specific design for my life, then my whole perspective about myself and the world changes radically!

Here's the problem. No human being was around when the universe began. All any of us know is what we are told by others. Most of us are told that we are nothing more than organized chaos and more developed "cousins" of the apes. But God has another story. He claims to be the Originator. He insists that He made all things and has specifically organized the universe for His glory and our benefit. That's what *The Book of Beginnings* is all about.

For since the creation of the world His invisible attributes are clearly seen, being understood by the things that are made, even His eternal power and Godhead (Romans 1:20).

Henry M. Morris III, D. Min.
Dallas, Texas

CHAPTER ONE
THE GENESIS CONTROVERSY

Genesis is a fascinating book! The timeless narratives contained in it have delighted spellbound youngsters since it was written. Scholars have debated the information for centuries—especially the historicity and authenticity of the first eleven chapters. Preachers have wrestled with the implications of the lives of the patriarchs. Countless readers have either gaped in awe at the power of God revealed in its pages or sneered at the idea that any "thinking" person could believe such nonsense.

One fact is clear: Genesis does not leave the reader in neutral.

The historical narratives are, of course, much more than timeless sources of interest, intrigue, and information. These inspired words of Scripture are the foundational "beginnings" of everything that God has undertaken on behalf of humanity. The language is easy to follow, uncomplicated, and rather plain. Compared to other "religious" books, Genesis is an unembellished, chronological record of our world—before there were many historians to record the events. It is indeed a book of beginnings.

That in itself ought to make Genesis required reading. Every teacher or person of influence should want to consider its foundational information before they decide how best to embrace their own perspective. That was the case in the Christian West for many centuries. The Bible stood as supreme literature and its pages were studied from earliest childhood through graduate training. No educated person would dare be caught ignorant of the historical thread of providential sovereignty, nor were the unread and untutored masses unaware of the Bible's main lessons. The book of Genesis was seen as essential to understanding the rest of the Bible.

Not so today.

Genesis has become, for some, the forgotten book. Its pages grow brittle from lack of use. Pastors and teachers grow ever more fearful of the controversy that *might* come from taking a public position. The result? Growing numbers of Christians are ignorant of God's revelation about our beginnings, and thus are either swayed by the atheistic alternative (that there is no beginning and no One who began it all), or they are stuck in a quagmire of confusion about their identity, their responsibility, and their future.

Why Is Genesis so Important?

Everybody "believes" in something. Even the atheist *believes* that there is no God—there is certainly no way to "prove" such a concept. Whether secular humanist or ardent Muslim, all men and women have "faith" in something—some "source" that expresses their presuppositions about who they are and why they are here.

The book of Genesis is the source for the Christian belief system.

The biblical record is *theistic* and *creationist*, while the Babylonian and subsequent Persian, Asian, Greek, and Roman cosmologies are either *pantheistic* or *polytheistic* but completely *evolutionary*. The theism of the early evolutionary religions either allowed worship of the various *personifications* of natural forces (polytheism), or the abstract *worship of Nature* (pantheism). The debate in the early millennia was not whether natural forces could "create" and "control" things. The debate was over whether the God of Scripture *created*, or the gods of Nature *perfected* the universe. The belief systems of humanity were not subjected to scientific (intellectual) evidences of proof as in today's predominantly secular environment, but rather to displays of power and demonstrations of prophetic accuracy.

Ideas Have Consequences

No human being operates without a bias—a predisposition to believe one idea over another. In religious terms we would call that bias "faith."

- What you **believe**, determines how you think.

- What you **think**, dictates what you do.

- What you **do**, dominates your life.

None but the most radical libertarian is comfortable with the global status quo. Politicians argue over a "cure" for the problems that plague society, but their solution is to treat the symptoms rather than attempting to discover the cause of the disease. The issues of human relationships have been abrogated to meaningless debates over techniques, programs, and economic distribution. The universal search for meaning has been reduced to nothing more than a search for a "fulfilling self-image," whatever that means. The Darwinian notion of the "survival of the fittest" has been encoded with the New Age jargon of self-empowerment. Women are seduced to purchase the most expensive hair care products because they are "worth it," while men are lured into drinking a certain beverage because it has more "gusto" than others.

The culture has been commercialized and customized, jingled and jangled, manipulated and motivated by innumerable proponents in every conceivable media with an inexhaustible supply of solutions. Happiness is always just around the corner. The reality is, however, that happiness is always temporary.

The timeless questions of humanity are often ignored.

- What is my purpose in life?

- Why is the world so full of evil?

- Why can't we all get along?

- Why can't we seem to get enough?

- Is it always going to be this way?

Much of what individuals embrace philosophically (and even religiously) does not require belief. The accepted clichés and jargon of one's particular cultural environment become substitutes for expressing *genuine* belief. Simply giving the "right answers" often brings social acceptance—in the business session, during the power lunch, along the halls of political influence, and even in the church fellowship hall. After we learn those answers, our life stabilizes until a crisis intervenes.

Then, what we believe takes over.

The book of Genesis is the basis for a biblical worldview. For no other reason than that, everyone who has an influential position among others ought to study, comprehend, and engage the message of this book of beginnings.

Who's in Charge?

As far as Genesis is concerned, the heart of the issue is *authority*. Is the Bible trustworthy or not? More importantly, is the Author of the Bible—God—trustworthy or not? If so, then God is supremely and exclusively authoritative on all matters about which He writes. If God is the Author of all truth and no untruth, then the very text of Scripture is purposefully and supernaturally inspired and trustworthy, even on matters of science.

The Scriptures are consistent.

God verifies, augments, describes, and cites His creative power without alteration throughout the Bible. Anyone who reads the record of Geneses *understands* what is written. The words and phrases are not at all complex to grasp, but they do require belief—for those words describe and present a Being whose power is limitless and whose knowledge is all-encompassing.

Neither you nor I can "experience" such a condition, and therefore we must either accept (believe) that there is an all-powerful and all-knowing God, transcendent to the universe, who is the First Cause of all things, or we must reject the existence of such a Being and retreat into our own experience and intelligence. Mankind, when confronted with that truth, must decide whether he will submit to the Author of that truth or reject both that truth and the Source of that truth—the Creator-God. There is no logical middle ground.

The bottom line, of course, is who rules? God? Or man?

The three monotheistic religions of the world—Judaism, Christianity, and Islam—are or were creationist at their core. They are theistic. These belief systems search for answers outside of nature. All other religions, derived in some measure from the Babylonian worship of the forces of nature, are or were evolutionary. They are naturalistic. These systems of belief seek to understand and explain all things in terms that are limited to natural phenomena and human interplay.

If God—the One who could speak the universe into existence with a command—is indeed the Creator, then He is the Owner of all that exists. Man is, therefore, a steward (rather than an owner) and is ultimately accountable to the Owner for all that is done with life and resources.

Who's Accountable?

A foundational principle of a creationist worldview is that man will answer to God.

On the other hand, if matter has always existed and random forces have been inexorably evolving upward, then humans are simply the best organisms that have been produced so far. Man, by default, becomes the owner of all he can rule. This is the overriding philosophy of naturalism—an atheistic-evolutionary, presuppositional belief system. There is no God (or "god" as in the forces of nature, or man himself). Nothing supernatural exists, except perhaps some "extra-terrestrial" race of super-intellects that have evolved in other parts of the universe. Since no evidence exists for the God of the Bible, man can be certain that there is no such thing as a "plan for your life." Man has reached the stage in time where he is able to direct the evolutionary development of the universe.

The creationist, on the other hand, believes that a Creator God exists and that God's creatures must seek to understand and carry out the will of the Creator.

What's the Difference?

The physical universe and all the information that humanity can uncover will be interpreted in the light of the belief system or worldview each individual holds. Even those mystics who believe in some form of reincarnation acknowledge that such "other lives" are unknown and are disconnected from present awareness, only surfacing in some kind of déjà vu experiences that are themselves not provable. To the naturalist, this life is all that there is. There is no future, no afterlife. When you're dead, you're dead!

Such hopeless beliefs drive many into lives of debauchery and hedonism, or fill the couches of psychologists and psychiatrists all over the world. Teenage suicide is alarmingly high, and therapists themselves continue to manifest one of the highest suicide rates in civilized countries. Scandals abound among the leaders of world business, politics, and even churches.

There is no "good news" in the evolutionary theory.

There is, however, glorious wonder and life-changing power in the "gospel" presented in the Bible. That message of salvation describes an eternal conversion from a spiritually dead and physically dying existence to spiritual eternal life now and a totally flawless "new heavens and new earth" in which those who are so "saved" will become both immortal and holy. How can such a thing be? Such a salvation must have *power*:

- power to transform now, in this life (Romans 12:2)

14

- power to enrich our current condition (2 Corinthians 9:11)

- power to bring satisfying peace to all situations (Hebrews 13:20-21)

- power to change the mortal body into the immortal and everlasting being who will live eternally with the Creator (1 Corinthians 15: 53-54)

But (and this is the point of this book) upon what is the "power" of the Good News based? Perhaps one can long for the changes promised and the beauty of eternal life spoken of in the pages of the Bible, but how can one believe such intangible promises unless there is some demonstration of the power necessary to defeat death and create new life?

Creation Involves Supernatural Power

While this may seem self-evident, some in Christian scholarship would not agree that God brought the universe into existence "out of nothing" during the creation event. Others have suggested that God was merely involved in the background or somehow operative in the natural forces that eventually produced the organized and functioning ability of nature.

The biblical text, however, is consistent in its record that there were omnipotent and omniscient acts of creation, that during the origin of our reality God "spoke, and it was done; He commanded, and it stood fast" (Psalm 33:9). The Scriptures also agree that during the creation week God also *made* and *shaped* that which He had *created* into an organized and functioning *cosmos*, which "was very good" (Genesis 1:31).

It would therefore follow that while man may well be able to understand the organization and function of the universe and "have dominion" over that which the Creator granted mankind stewardship, man will not be able to understand, explain, manipulate, or control that which was not made out "of things which do appear" (Hebrews 11:3). Or as another Bible writer puts it, God "calls those things which do not exist as though they did" (Romans 4:17).

The Necessity of Written Revelation

Man can, through diligence and careful attention to detail, un-cover much about the things "made" and "shaped" by God during creation. Indeed, man was given the authority to "rule" and "subdue" the earth by his Creator, and those disciplines that we call science and technology are the methods by which we uncover much evidence for the functioning of the creation. But the "how" of the beginnings remains far beyond a finite mind. To believe that such knowledge is obtainable is to believe man can obtain equality with the Creator.

The insatiable drive to achieve such equality would be inexpli-cable apart from the event of rebellion against the Creator recorded in Genesis. Those who shared an open relationship with the Creator, i.e., Adam and Eve, were willing to risk death to acquire "evil" knowledge, so that they could "be like God" (Genesis 3:5).

The idea that the Creator used power, processes, and program-ming, for which we have neither current knowledge nor the ability to gain such knowledge, makes many people very angry. Why? Because the Bible insists that man's mind is both corrupt and powerless to grasp the creating power of God. Denying that limitation has become the rallying cry around which a majority of humanity has become united. "God" may exist, some might declare, but *if* he does, he is absolutely removed from any involvement in human affairs.

Consider the fact that those who reject Genesis 1:1—that God created anything at all—have by every means possible sought to dis-prove this fact. Naturalism is the archenemy of this concept. Dar-winian evolution has as its chief presupposition the disbelief of God and creation. It is certainly clear from such passages as Psalm 19:1-4 and Romans 1:18-25 that God created the universe to "speak" and "declare" and "show" much of His nature. And although the creation declares and speaks of God's glory, the "law of the LORD is perfect, converting the soul; the testimony of the LORD is sure, making wise the simple; the statutes of the LORD are right, rejoicing the heart; the commandment of the LORD is pure, enlightening the eyes; the fear of the LORD is clean, enduring forever; the judgments of the LORD are true and righteous altogether" (Psalm 19:7-9).

That which is created tells us something about the nature of the Creator.

Revealed words define, clarify, limit, and command. The text of the Bible is that which is inspired and as such is "profitable for doctrine, for reproof, for correction, for instruction in righteousness, that the man of God may be complete, thoroughly equipped for every good work" (2 Timothy 3:16-17).

Natural revelation—created things—would, therefore, provide only limited insight into truth. Final authority would rest in the written revelation that God "breathed" into a "living" record (1 Peter 1:23) that "shall not pass away" (Mark 13:31). It should follow then that one can only understand the events of creation by revelation, not by discovery. Science cannot duplicate or comprehend creation. Man can merely steward or manage that which is held together by the Creator in longsuffering mercy (2 Peter 3:8-9).

The main proponents of evolutionary naturalism and the associated sociological exponents of that philosophy are atheistic in thinking if not in practice. Modernism, postmodernism, and the many variations of scientism are united in their opposition to the concept of a transcendent Creator God. The very idea of an omnipotent, omniscient Supreme Being is anathema to naturalistic concepts of existence.

The myriad pantheistic and polytheistic religious and spiritual "isms" of history, as well as the New Age proponents of today, all embrace some concept of the existence of eternal matter with long ages and gradual development of the universe and life. Interestingly, the academic world has begun to entertain "spiritual" interpretations of naturalistic science as the evidence for complexity and design grows more and more obvious. Yet most academics still cling to evolutionary cosmologies because they cannot accept an omnipotent and omniscient Creator.

Handling the actual texts of Scripture, then, becomes fundamentally important. Are the written words of the book of Genesis to be treated as historical narrative? Are the biblical writers who comment on the creation account to be taken literally? What does "inspiration" require? What liberties are allowed in "interpreting" the text? Do extrabiblical data have superiority over the text? Should the words, the context, and the multiple passages that give the same message be taken at face value, or is there liberty to alter the understanding of what is written in order to conform to some other standard?

While a sizeable portion of Christianity does not endorse any sort of plenary, verbal view of inspiration, these discussions will insist that the words of Scripture—God's words—hold sway over the opinions and musings of those who do not believe that God has revealed absolute, unalterable truth.

All conservative evangelical leaders would appear to agree that the biblical context sets the primary stage for meaning and application of the text. All appear to agree that the specific structure of the syntax must be subject to the axiomatic truths of the rest of Scripture. Very few would suggest that God "lies" or "accommodates" His Word in any way to human error, but some would allow for divergent meanings from the apparent rendering of the text (e.g., "day" = "age"). Some would suggest that the words of the text should be "interpreted" and/or "filtered" by various extra-biblical methods and standards.

If all the writings—the Scriptures—are God-breathed, then upon what authority can change be made to the apparent meaning of the words? Upon what basis is the text to be deconstructed or reconstructed? If *some* of the Bible's words can be subjected to the currency of science or theology or scholarship, what authority determines *which* words will be changed? If some of the words can be subjected to human disciplines, then what standard is used to determine the extent to which the subjugation applies?

To whom or what is entrusted the responsibility of determining what God "breathed" and what He did not? Upon what basis is the trust determined? What specialized training from which institutions are required to become responsible to make this determination? Are only God's *thoughts* (i.e., dynamic principles, ideas) authorized by God? Are God's thoughts not made up of words? Can man understand God's "breath" without His words? What standards must we use (if not the words themselves) to train others to "searched the scriptures daily, whether those things were so" (Acts 17:11)?

If the Lord Be God, Follow Him

Once again, the heart of the issue is *authority*. Is the Bible trustworthy or not? More importantly, is the Author of the Bible—God—trustworthy or not? If so, then God is supremely and exclusively authoritative on all matters about which He writes.

In other words, if God is the Author of all truth and not *un*truth, then the very text of Scripture is purposefully and supernaturally inspired and trustworthy, even on matters of science. Mankind, when faced with truth, must decide whether he will submit to the Author of truth or reject both the truth and the God who insists that His word is Truth. There is no middle ground or compromise.

More particularly, the Christian must decide what constitutes his authority when reading and communicating the truth of Scripture. The Bible or science? The Author of the Bible or the experts in science? Again, there is no neutral position.

The Dominant Worldviews

Two belief systems or worldviews now stand at the center of reflective and deductive thought. One seeks to understand and explain all things in terms limited to natural phenomena and human interplay. The other finds naturalistic explanations unsatisfactory and searches for answers outside of nature in the supernatural realm.

Naturalism that is secular and humanistic

According to this belief system, all supernatural influence is eliminated by evolutionary thought; only observable natural processes exist. Since man is the dominant life form, he alone controls his destiny and directs the progress of the universe. Since the destiny of the universe is held in the hands of men, mankind and the knowledge he produces (i.e., science) become the objects of highest respect (i.e., worship).

In a nutshell, atheistic naturalism posits that random processes over unimaginable time have brought into existence the human race. Mankind now is the epitome of self-determining matter, and as such is the only "salvation" that the planet can depend on for survival. There is no "god." There is no "afterlife." Man's highest goal for himself is survival as long as possible—and to enjoy his existence to its fullest while it lasts.

Naturalism that is polytheistic or pantheistic

Whereas Western thought has moved toward either theism or atheism, much of the non-Western world remains steeped in animism or a mixture of new and old pagan philosophies. Ancient cultures exchanged the worship of God (Jehovah) for the worship of nature (cf. Romans 1). Various aspects of the natural world—sun, moon, stars, wind, water, earth, etc.—were personified and became objects of worship because of the supposed "supernatural" forces they displayed. Buddhism and Hinduism mixed pagan animism with humans or human-like creatures to symbolize man's relation to the supernatural.

Man's physical and spiritual ascent to deity through these religions became the central theme. New Age philosophies have essentially modernized old pagan beliefs with sophisticated packaging and Madison Avenue promotional campaigns.

The result is the same: Nature becomes a god (or gods) as determined by mankind. Thus, mankind becomes the architect of deity.

Biblical theism and creationism

The theism of the pantheist or the polytheist is still both naturalist and evolutionary. Although those aberrations of a theistic perspective deify the forces, the practical effect is still naturalism and, ultimately, atheistic.

The message of the Bible, beginning at the very first verse of the book of Genesis, is that there is only one Deity. That unique Being has, of His own authority, power, and knowledge, brought our reality into existence. That Deity is transcendent and sovereign over that which He created, and has delegated functional responsibility to humanity for the development and progress of that which was created.

During the millennia that have passed since creation, mankind has gone through many stages of "belief" or "rebellion" and now is living among a global milieu of nations and social structures that are essentially dominated by the tensions between an acknowledgment (if not submission to) of a "creator" and the intellectual elite of the world who have tried for over three centuries to abolish such "idealism" from the consciousness of the general population.

In the "Christian" West, the churches range from a formal liturgical system steeped in traditionalism to a ribald emotionalism with seemingly no moorings at all. Within that vast range of Christian thought are those who would attempt to blend secular humanism and evolutionary philosophies with favored messages from Scripture. Even the most "literal" of the Bible-based theological systems struggle with the sociological, scientific, and political messages of the last 200 years.

Yet, however strong the effort to mix the messages, the opposing worldviews are not designed to be united in any way. They are, by their very core nature, diametrically opposed.

The clearest contrast of these worldviews can be seen in the language and perspectives used to shape social mores. The resulting radical shift in morals and ethics observed during the past three decades in most countries may best be understood when contrasting today's naturalistic framework with the biblical perspective.

SOCIOLOGICAL FRAMEWORK	BIBLICAL FRAMEWORK
Moral Relativism	**Moral Absolutes**
Every principle, every choice of lifestyle is reduced to personal preference.	God has spoken and delivered His standards. These standards do not change.
Multiculturalism	**Cultural Diversity**
All cultures and lifestyles are morally equivalent and equally affirmed.	All cultural practices are judged by God's truth. All individuals need a Savior.
Pragmatism	**Idealism**
Actions and policies are judged by effectiveness.	God's standards are revealed and absolute for every action and policy.
Utopianism	**Eschatological Hope**
Human nature is basically good and will achieve perfection through man's efforts.	Human nature is sinful. Only God redeems and brings about righteousness.
This-World Perspective	**Eternal Perspective**
This universe is "all there is." There is no supernatural being or other reality.	This universe will be destroyed and then renewed in perfection by its Creator.

Man's Hybrid Theories

There are several forms of this divergence. Some would suggest that God uses the natural forces inherent in our present world to "create" over time (Theistic Evolution). Others would suggest that God has intervened with *ex nihilo* acts of creation during the natural progression of evolutionary development (Progressive Creation). Still others would take a neutral stance on these issues, suggesting that the details and mechanisms are either unimportant or irrelevant to the overall message that God is the Creator—however He did it.

Several common threads run among these alternatives to *ex nihilo* creation.

Reason has become superior to the text of Scripture

Man's intellect is now used to explain away the inconsistencies between the biblical text and the doctrines of naturalism. Articulate spokesmen have garnered large followings. Deconstruction of biblical words have become commonplace, with new systems of theology being generated to promulgate the error. "Dynamic translations" and "culturally relevant" editions of the Bible are replacing scholarly efforts to translate from the original texts. God's words have become God's thoughts, and these thoughts are open to "interpretation" and "relevant application." The personalized meaning of Scripture has become more important a filter than the linguistic definition or the clear words of the context.

Experience substitutes for the doctrines of God's Word

- The ideology of personal freedom has become so widespread that restrictions on lifestyle are rarely preached, and much has happened in the church to encourage an adaptation of the gospel message to cultural mores. Visions of greatness, dreams for the future, creative intuition, and personal experiences have supplanted the written Word.

- "Wrong" is only that which causes pain.

- "Right" is that which feels good and bring happiness.

- "Fun" is sought in the place of "joy."

Sex has become a "recreation" granted by God for personal fulfillment, not the "procreation" responsibility of one man and one woman.

Since man is at liberty to do as he pleases, then he is free to override anything that conflicts with his wishes.

Pragmatism succeeds theology

The evangelical world has elevated the concept of personal acceptance to a finely-tuned church growth process. Sermons are couched in "seeker" terms, evangelism has deteriorated to the drawing of unsaved to events, and Christian maturity has become equated with a positive attitude and possibility thinking. That which produces the largest crowd is copied and developed into books and seminars and television shows. The most effective return on the dollar has driven a per-pew, per-person, per-service analysis of every method, event, and process within the walls. That which works has become that which is true.

Science is placed over Scripture

Over the past 150 years since Darwin popularized the notion of evolution, the academic world has come to embrace evolutionary naturalism. That phenomenon is not new by any stretch of the imagination, but what has become a more pressing issue is that many evangelical scholars are embracing Darwinian hybrid theories.

That movement in the Western world began among the more liberal seminaries during the late 1800s and early 1900s and has spawned various theories of creation:

- Theistic Evolution

- The "Gap" Theory

- The "Day-Age" Theory

- Analogical Days or Progressive Creation
- Framework Interpretation of Scripture

Modern science must be accommodated

Assumed in all of the various hybrid creation alternatives is the verifiability of eons of time for the existence of the universe and earth. Since, it is reasoned, modern science has proven that the earth is billions of years old, theologians must therefore interpret the text of Genesis (and other relevant passages) to harmonize with that age.

Although some earlier theologians would merely relegate the "ages" to an unknown "gap" between the first two verses of Genesis, most scholars would embrace some form of a Day-Age interpretation of the first chapter, with subsequent modifications of parallel information throughout the Scriptures.

Implied and often openly embraced with the long ages is the corollary accommodation of evolutionary development over those long ages. Naturalistic interpretations of present reality require billions of incomprehensible time periods to allow for evolutionary progression. Any age-long interpretation of the creation account in Genesis would necessarily permit an evolutionary scheme to fit easily within it.

The age issue must be resolved

Physical death is considered normal and part of God's "good" creative acts. With the exception of the older Gap Theory, physical death is seen as a normal and regular part of the "days" of the creation week. The Gap Theory suggests that a pre-Adamic world was destroyed by God, leaving a record of that judgment in the rocks of the earth. All the various hybrid interpretations (including the Gap Theory) would view the fossil record as evidence of the death of enormous numbers of life forms *prior* to the creation of Adam and Eve.

This divergence is more far-reaching theologically than the suggestion that the "days" may be "ages." Not only is the meaning of the word "death" in question, but the entire body of biblical data on the substitutionary atonement is impacted. Many of the textual terms surrounding the Fall, the Flood, the Crucifixion, the Resurrection, and the ultimate destruction of death and the elimination of the Curse, appear to become free-floating concepts when the anchor of the apparent meaning of death is removed.

The Flood of Noah could not have been global

If one accepts the textual language of Genesis 6-9 as accurate, historical language, meant to be taken at face value, then the scientific and geological implications are enormous. If "all" air-breathing life died, if "all" the high hills were covered, and the waters "increased" for 150 days, requiring over one year to drain sufficiently for Noah and those with him in the Ark to disembark, then the Flood described would have left a worldwide record visible for all to see. Indeed, if such a visible record is demonstrable, then modern geology, and therefore long-age evolutionary interpretation of the fossil record, would be radically affected.

Thus, all old-age hybrid interpretations of the Genesis record must treat the biblical record of Noah's Flood as some form of regional or local inundation that merely impacted the known world—primarily the Mesopotamian valley in the Fertile Crescent region of ancient civilizations. However, if the Flood was global, then the worldwide catastrophe would have laid down most of the sedimentary layers and the fossils they contain in one year—not over hundreds of millions of years.

Such a contrast and conflict cannot be resolved unless the biblical record is interpreted to meet the scientific criteria, or the science is interpreted to fit the biblical text. Evangelical scholarship cannot have it both ways. Either the biblical text is superior to naturalistic interpretations of geological data, or the naturalistic interpretation of geological data is superior to the biblical text.

Evolutionary naturalism opposes the revealed character of God

It is no academic secret that the main proponents of evolutionary naturalism and the associated sociological exponents of that philosophy are atheistic in theory if not in practice, such as modernism, post-modernism, and various forms of scientism—all of which are opposed to the idea of a Creator.

Such an evolutionary philosophy is in diametric opposition to the revealed text of Scripture. A "god" who would use the cruel, inefficient, wasteful, death-filled processes of the random, purposeless mechanisms of naturalistic evolution, contrasts so radically with the God described in the pages of the Bible, that one wonders how the two characters can ever be thought to be in harmony.

The wedge of Intelligent Design

Intermingled initially among Progressive Creationists, and now a movement in its own right, are the efforts of Intelligent Design theorists. The motives of the leaders of the ID movement seem to be more idealistic and pure than the compromise attempts of previous theories. While the other "isms" tried to make the Bible say something it clearly does not say, these writers insist that empirical science alone demonstrates such overwhelming evidence for "design" that logic would dictate the necessity for a "Designer."

Unlike the Progressive, Gap, and Theistic Evolution writers, however, proponents of the ID movement make the conscious choice to stay away from biblical arguments and concentrate only on scientific data. As such, their efforts initially met with more appreciation and acceptance from secular science since they did not attempt to force the Bible into the equation.

However, and this is a big "however," by insisting on leaving God out and hoping that pure logic will lead others to conclude that God is the Designer behind the design, the ID proponents have left out the power of the gospel (Romans 1:16). Committed evolutionists have not capitulated to the logic of these "design" arguments. More dangerously, some mystic thinkers have embraced the ID concept, trying to milk the wave of Christian acceptance to feed various Christianized brands of "cosmic consciousness."

Taking God Out of the Message Will Ultimately Lead to Human Error

The common denominator running among all of these various hybrid systems of interpretation is the elevation of man's "discoveries" over and above the words of God. The most elemental example of faith is God's omnipotent and omniscient authority displayed in His creation (Hebrews 11:3). The matrix in which modern science is enmeshed is atheistic, naturalistic evolution. The Bible puts man's "natural" mind in direct juxtaposition and diametric opposition to the Spirit's revelation (1 Corinthians 2:14). To insist that the revelation of a supernatural creation must be wedded with a naturalistic and evolutionary god, flies in the face of the whole of Scripture (Romans 1:20).

These issues are not merely choices of a favored method of interpretation, but a frontal assault on the opening declaration of God. Stripped of their "science" and "literary criticism," these theologies are dangerous denigrations of who God is and what He has revealed.

> Remember the former things of old, For I am God, and there is no other; I am God, and there is none like Me, declaring the end from the beginning, And from ancient times things that are not yet done, Saying, "My counsel shall stand, And I will do all My pleasure." (Isaiah 46:9-10)

Genesis—book of beginnings—is the introduction to that God. Rejecting any of its record will both undermine the understanding of the rest of God's revelation, and also slowly dissolve one's confidence in the biblical message itself and discourage any thought of establishing or maintain a relationship with the God of that Bible.

CHAPTER TWO
THE BEGINNING OF THE UNIVERSE

Efforts to define "the beginning" have occupied human culture as long as written records have documented the thinking of past history. Myth and legend abound throughout the long trail of people groups in our world. The most simple and profound statement ever recorded is this: "In the beginning, God created the heavens and the earth" (Genesis 1:1). Many other "stories" have been uncovered over the centuries from the ancient Babylonian *Enuma Elish* to the myriad records of ethnic groups all over the planet. All of these varied accounts have several points in common.

- The "beginning" was long ago
- The state of the initial universe was dark and chaotic
- The energies involved were supernatural
- The ordering of the chaos was also supernatural
- The plant and animal life preceded man
- The paradise of the original world was lost
- The first age was destroyed by a flood

But, as the popular cliché goes, "the devil is in the details." Even though the big pieces of the many myths and legends appear to fit the

Bible record fairly well, as any one even remotely familiar with the basic arguments knows, the difference in the details is both vast and contradictory.

When Was "The Beginning"?

Before examining the many differences in the ideas about the origin of the universe, it is necessary to ask the question: "How do we determine when the beginning actually began?" Surely the reader will be aware that the majority opinion of modern science is that the universe is between 18 and 20 billion years old. That does, at least in principle, agree with most of the other myths and legends that have been documented—except the information in the book of beginnings—the book of Genesis. If general consensus is to be the ruling factor in this very important question, then a rational person would lean toward accepting the "deep time" of the evolutionary system of thinking.

The majority opinion

All of the non-biblical ideas about the beginning start with the assumption of long eons of chaotic development. Some suggest an eternal revolving "ying and yang" that oscillates between chaos and order over unthinkable ages of time. Most of Western science, however, asserts that all the energy of the existing universe was once concentrated into a very small ball, which suddenly and spontaneously exploded billions of years ago. They call that event the Big Bang, and consider it to be the "beginning" of our universe.

Essentially, the scientist plugs in numbers for the variables in the formula, and then tries to solve the equation. Differences exist over what the numbers are and what the variables should be, but agreement is shared on the main points: something with vast mass-energy exploded long ago and set off processes that produced stars, galaxies, and planets. Our earth and solar system somehow coalesced out of the cosmic debris generated by the Big Bang. That happened, it is asserted, between 4.5 and 5 billion years ago.

Not all evolutionary thinkers embrace the Big Bang, but many do.

It certainly is the most popular of the current theories. This concept uses Einstein's General Theory of Relativity to explain a few of the major observations that we see in the universe and primarily "proves" itself from a set of mathematical equations that are devised to explain the idea. The "proof" of the Big Bang is based on circular thinking: "I think the universe got started from an explosion long ago. Here is the math that will explain how I think that happened."

Quite a few otherwise evolutionary scientists do not agree with this "logic."

> The BIG BANG theory relies on a growing number of hypothetical entities—things that we have never observed. Inflation, dark matter and dark energy are the most prominent. Without them, there would be fatal contradictions between the observations made by astronomers and the predictions of the big bang theory. In no other field of physics would this continual recourse to new hypothetical objects be accepted as a way of bridging the gap between theory and observation. It would, at the least, raise serious questions about the validity of the underlying theory.[1]

> I don't expect the vast majority of astronomers to pay the slightest attention to Hoyle and his colleagues: frankly, there are too many careers riding on the Big Bang being right.[2]

> Plasma cosmology and the steady-state model both hypothesize an evolving universe without beginning or end.[3]

Scientists who are committed to naturalism do not believe in any type of supernatural agency or event intervening in the development of the universe. Such scientists are at least consistent in their atheistic and evolutionary explanations.

---

1. Eric J. Lerner, Bucking the Big Bang, *New Scientist,* May 22, 2004, 20.
2. Robert Matthews, Sir Fred Returns to Give Big Bang Another Kicking, *Sunday Telegraph,* February 13, 2000.
3. Lerner, Bucking the Big Bang, 20.

However, and this may sound extreme, a scientist who insists that he believes the biblical record but then uses the Big Bang to justify his departure from the clear text of Scripture is no different than a peasant who sees the Virgin Mary appear in the dust of the road or in grease clinging to the wall. The process is exactly the same: personal experience and belief substitute and superimpose themselves on the tangible evidence. The peasant may well have a better excuse; he is usually untaught. Rarely does he know what the Word of God teaches, and God may be more forgiving of his zeal. But the Christian scholar, one who has studied the Bible and takes pains to search the biblical text for those words that can be made to fit his version of the truth, that person is in far more danger from God's judgment than the peasant.

Is the universe eternal?

All of the "creation" stories other than the Genesis record suggest that there was eternal matter in some form. Some think that the primeval form was water, while others speak of various eternal "gods" or "forces" of some kind. Modern naturalistic science tends to embrace talk about an unimaginably dense "speck" (some form of hydrogen-mass-energy) from which the present universe formed after this speck exploded. Of course, no one really knows if that is so, but *something* has to be *the source* from which all that exists originated!

Since "eternal" matter sounds too much like mythology to the modern ear, it is generally accepted that the universe is somewhere between 18 and 20 billions of years old. Even though that age has grown over the decades to satisfy modern astronomy, all evolutionary and naturalistic science agrees on an ancient universe. The proof most often cited are the light years distance of the uncounted stars and galaxies.

What about the light years?

It's important to remember that this term designates *distance*, not *time*. Here are the facts. Light travels approximately 299,792,458 meters per second or approximately 186,282 miles per second (as we have been able to measure the speed on earth). Zipping along at that speed for 60 seconds for one minute, continuing for 60 minutes over one hour for 24 hours each day, 365.25 days during the year, light would travel 5,877,981,691,000 miles over that one year. Hence, when a physicist or an astronomer speaks of a star being 3.5 "light years" away, he is talking about the *distance* that the object is from our planet, *not* how long it took light to get here.

Oh, yes, everybody *assumes* that the distance is equal to the time—but that part of the equation has not yet been proven. In fact much of Einstein's famous General Theory of Relativity is built around the variability of time, space, and matter. Thousands of pages have been written wrangling over the time-space problems, but the problem has not yet been solved—"science" hasn't gotten very far.

What has been agreed to by naturalistic scientists, however, is that the universe cannot be young in any sense of that word. But, there really is no proof (test) that can demonstrate the "deep time" so desperately needed for the plausibility of "natural" causes for our reality. All who reject the biblical model *must* "believe" in long ages. No other scenario could suggest that the current processes that we now observe and upon which we now depend would have enough time to "evolve" from something less (simple) to that which exists.

In simple language: Earth and its ecosystems and its people groups exist. Our earth is functioning very nicely under rather clear natural laws. Those laws (physics, chemistry, biology, etc.) are really quite stable. Since it is "believed" that there has been no supernatural "creation" or "non-natural" force ever operating in our universe, the processes necessary to produce what we now can observe and measure must provide the scale and mathematical models by which we can project backwards to the time when these various elements and processes might have begun.

Therefore, since "the present is the key to the past," mankind develops "stories" about how things began and then more stories about how our reality progressed from the most simple of energies to the vast complex of galaxies, planets, ecosystems, life-forms, nations, and people groups. And all of this *must* ultimately be embraced by scholarship, politicians, scientists, and global industry if a "New World Order" is to usher in a "New Age" of peace and prosperity. Man *must* have such a story if he is to deceive both himself and all who reject the clear, simple, and factual texts of Genesis.

Why Is Age Such an Important Question?

Incomprehensible ages make evolution seem possible. Over *billions* of years, anything can happen. Right? It is impossible to test, but relatively easy to construct the story. The Bible clearly teaches a young earth, created by an omnipotent God. If one can destroy the Bible's credibility, it then becomes easy to deny the Bible's Creator. When science becomes the factor by which we approve or filter the information available to us (including the Bible record)—man becomes the judge.

> The secrets of evolution are death and time—the deaths of enormous numbers of lifeforms that were imperfectly adapted to the environment; and time for a long succession of small mutations that were by accident adaptive, time for the slow accumulation of patterns of favorable mutations.[4]

In practical terms, "billions" of anything is impossible to grasp. Billions of years might as well be eternal—and the immense eons are absolutely necessary to make the evolutionary "story" sound plausible. Any thinking person would scoff at chemical "goop" becoming a living organism in a few thousand years through random activity—but given billions of years, anything seems possible.

> Time is in fact the hero of the plot....Given so much time, the "impossible" becomes possible, and the possible probable, and the probable virtually certain. One has only to wait; time itself performs miracles.[5]

This premise is absolutely vital to the concept of the naturalistic

---

4. Carl Sagan, 1980, *Cosmos,* New York: Random House, 30.
5. George Wald, The Origin of Life, in *The Physics and Chemistry of Life,* New York: Simon and Schuster, 12.

explanation of everything. If the universe is young (thousands instead of billions), then the idea of natural processes randomly producing the vast array of complex matter in the universe is unthinkable.

Herein lies the core of the problem.

As we try to grasp the meaning of our existence, we are inevitably led to seek answers about the origin of everything. That quest always bumps up against the unknown. Science is supposed to be about that which we can observe—or at least about that which we can test our ideas about what we do not observe. The so called *scientific method* demands that our observations should lead us to form *theories* that we test by very restricted (and observable) processes. If our test verifies our theories, then we use the knowledge gained to pry more deeply into the various aspects of our reality.

But, when our theories require testing procedures that we either cannot devise or cannot understand, then we are left with concepts that are purely hypothetical (e.g., the Big Bang), which we then try to "prove" by various mathematical models and formulae that themselves are both debatable and un-provable.

Indeed, man is quite capable of inventing stories of "how things came to be." He is also capable of writing volumes of explanations, in very scholarly words, with lots of math and tables and charts that "show" what he means—but these musings are still stories and not science! There may be a sprinkling of various facts within the musings, but those facts are applied to a resulting theory that has nothing to do with the facts being used.

Many clock-like processes operating in the solar system and beyond indicate that the universe is young. For example, spiral galaxies should not exist if they are billions of years old. The stars near their centers rotate around the galactic cores faster than stars at the perimeters. If a cosmology based on long ages is correct, they should have blended into disk-shaped galaxies by now.

Comets pose a similar problem. They lose material each time they pass around the sun. Why would they still exist after vast eons? Saturn's rings still look new and shiny. And many planets and moons are geologically very active. Surely the energy they continually expend should have been spent long ago if they are as old as they are usually claimed to be.

Instead, the more astronomers learn about the heavens, the more evidence there is that the universe is young.

In the biblical record there is not a hint of unknown ages.

The basic conflict

Ultimately, we are faced with a conflict of process—creation *ex nihilo* by fiat within six 24-hour days, or "creation" over vast ages, using natural forces of random evolutionary development that inexorably progress from the simple to the complex.

In the one, God brings into existence a cosmos (a universe of ordered structure) with functional maturity designed to fulfill His sovereign plan for the ages.

In the other, blind nature orchestrates purely natural processes, allowing them to evolve toward new stages or events or processes that come into existence. These new events ultimately lead to a dominant life form (man) that can control and direct its own evolution.

How can we know?

The only means of really *knowing* anything about "the beginning" is by revelation. God was there. He knows. No human scientist or historian was there when the universe began. Evolutionary speculations of many varieties have abounded throughout human history, and some have formed the mythological basis of various religions. But they were all obtained either by human imagination or by supernatural deception.

The modern evolutionary story—Darwinism—has served as the scientific rationale for the religions of atheism, socialism, humanism, fascism, and even laissez-fair capitalism and imperialism, but it also is without any factual foundation.

The only way we can truly *know* anything about creation is for the Creator to tell us. Creation is not occurring now (that's the same problem as the evolutionary theories), so we cannot study the process in operation. In fact, the present processes of the universe are all conservative in nature, operating in concert with the two most widely established "laws" of science. Basically, those laws tell us that all mass-energy is stable in quantity (no creation or destruction going on), but unstable in quality (everything deteriorates over time). So far as we can know, those two laws have always been operating through history. Therefore, there is no possible way that they can tell us about creation—except that "the beginning" must have happened in the past by creative processes no longer operating.

The Biblical Alternative

However, the text of the biblical record is so different, both in style and substance, that one is at least cautioned to carefully consider its alternative message before blithely embracing either the mythological stories or the scientific ones.

Consider the fact that those who reject Genesis 1:1—that God created anything at all—have by every means possible sought to disprove this fact. Naturalism is the archenemy of this concept. Darwinian evolution has as its chief presupposition the disbelief of God and creation. The Christian who seeks to genuinely understand the creation account will discover that the truths in the first two chapters of Genesis are, to a certain extent, not difficult to grasp. The Holy Spirit and faith in the Creator are the foundation (Hebrews 11:1-3) for a thorough and enlightened study. As a result, the believer is encouraged in his own faith and prepared to offer a solid defense of the creation account to those who ask (1 Peter 3:15).

The ordinary reading of Genesis 1 is clear. God created the world and all it contains in six 24-hour days. The language could not be more precise. The light portion is called "day" and the dark portion is called "night." Each numbered day (1st day, 2nd day, 3rd day, etc.) is defined as having an "evening and a morning." The obvious understanding of this text has been without dispute for millennia by believers and detractors alike. Those who held to the pagan systems of "creation" and their long-age chaos stories of "gods and goddesses" simply rejected the Bible text as wrong. No attempt was made to "interpret" the obvious language.

The language of the Bible

The book of Genesis was originally written in the Hebrew language, as was the rest of the Old Testament (with a few passages written in Aramaic). While it is not necessary to become fluent in biblical Hebrew, it will be helpful to understand key Hebrew terms used in the creation account, especially in light of the level of debate associated with these terms. It is also helpful to note textual elements such as the grammar and genre of the Genesis record.

First, the languages in which the Bible was written are far more vivid and meaningful than translations can express. Word studies, therefore, become an essential part of Bible study. There are many helps available today, both in print and with computer software programs. Most of these can bring out the various nuances of the original language rather easily. To be sure, several of the English translations are excellent and convey the meanings of the biblical text accurately. But the process of examining the language for certain key terms will often reveal a fuller meaning from the text.

Second, please understand that God did not go through all the effort of inspiring Scripture over such long periods of time to make the interpretations available only to Ph.D.s and seminary-trained theologians. On the contrary, the primary reason for the revelation of God's Word was to communicate history and truth and instruction and wisdom to the world—and ultimately to those who would believe Him.

Grammar and genre

The grammatical structure of Genesis 1-2 clearly falls within *narrative* genre. This is an account—a historical record—similar to those found in the other portions of the Old Testament where the writer describes people and places and events and time. The sentence structure—subject, verb, object, etc.—is consistent with the narrative style. Also, there is no indication in the text that the creation account is to be read as an allegory or in any figurative manner. This is a report of what actually happened. The writer does not say "…it was as if God created something like a great light in the heavens…." The common-sense approach to study is the best approach. That is, read and inter-pret the passage as it appears.

For example, the Psalms are written as poetry or lyrics. There are Hebrew parallelisms, frequent repetitions of words or phrases, and many more descriptive words to convey emotions as well as facts. The Psalms are intended to be read (or sung) in just this fashion. The prophetic books are replete with predictive text and announcements, sometimes in the form of visions and dreams and unusual illustrative stories. Often the reader is told the interpretation of these visions, thus indicating how one is to discover the meaning of the text.

But the historical books of the Old Testament are just that—his-tory. They are read and understood as "chronicles" of what took place in certain places to certain people at certain times with certain results. And this is exactly the structure of the creation account and Genesis as a whole. It is a chronicle of what God was doing for the first seven days of the universe, and then what happened to His newly created world.

Not one human was present when God created anything recorded in Genesis 1. In fact, it is possible that God Himself recorded the ac-count of creation and gave it to Adam (perhaps on stone tablets), who would pass the records down to succeeding generations. To consider the beginning of all things—the beginning of matter itself—is to con-template the unknowable.

> For My thoughts are not your thoughts, nor are your ways My ways," says the LORD. "For as the heavens are higher than the earth, so are My ways higher than your ways, and My thoughts than your thoughts. (Isaiah 55:8-9)

Indeed, not even the most gifted and God-fearing theologian or scientist can adequately explain the beginning of all things. However, God in His grace revealed to mankind in the Scriptures all that is necessary to know about creation.

Three Key Verbs

The Holy Spirit, the "breath" of God who has "inspired" (2 Timothy 3:16) the writing of the Bible, used three specific and very different action words to describe and define what God did during the creation week. Understanding the import of these terms will clarify the events of the creation week and provide insight into the character of the Creator.

Bārā'

"In the beginning God created...." The word "created" is translated from the Hebrew word *bārā'* and means to create, shape, or fashion. Only God is the subject when this word is used in the Bible. *Bārā'* is used two other times in Genesis 1, describing the creation of animals with consciousness or life (v. 21) and the creation of mankind (v. 27). There are five other occurrences in Genesis where *bārā'* is used (Genesis 2:3-4; 5:1-2; 6:7).

Bārā' is used on Day One, Day Five, and Day Six.

One of the consistent observations in the first chapter of Genesis is that God "said" (spoke) when He caused something to happen. The "speaker"—we find out later in the biblical record—is none other than the second Person of the Trinity, the Lord Jesus Christ.

> In the beginning was the Word, and the Word was with God, and the Word was God. He was in the beginning with God. All things were made through Him, and without Him nothing was made that was made. (John 1:1-3)

> And the Word became flesh and dwelt among us, and we beheld His glory, the glory as of the only begotten of the Father, full of grace and truth. (John 1:14)

The Greek term for "Word" is *logos*, and as John 1:14 insists, this *Logos* is the Lord Jesus. He was the person of the Godhead responsible for calling "all things" into existence. The Latin term *ex nihilo* is often used to describe this concept—bringing something into existence out of nothing. According to the biblical text, there was no eternal matter from which everything else was made. All that existed before creation was God Himself.

> ...God, who gives life to the dead and calls those things which do not exist as though they did. (John 4:17)

> By faith we understand that the worlds were framed by the word of God, so that the things which are seen were not made of things which are visible. (Hebrews 11:3)

One must choose either to believe in an eternal God or in "eternal" matter.

'Asah

"Thus God made..." (Genesis 1:7). The word "made" is the Hebrew *'asah* and means to do, fashion, accomplish, make, organize, structure, etc. It is used throughout the creation account, beginning in Genesis 1:7 (Genesis 1:11, 12, 16, 25, 26, 31; 2:2, 3, 4). While *'asah* is sometimes used interchangeably with *bārā'* in Genesis 1, it is not used exclusively of God's creative activity. It is used on Day Two, Day Three, and Day Four of the creation week (Genesis 1:7, 11, 16).

'Asah is used 140 times in the book of Genesis. It is a very common verb, used widely to describe "doing" or "making" something. Genesis 3:7 is the first instance of *'asah* used with man as the "maker."

> Then the eyes of both of them were opened, and they knew that they were naked; and they sewed fig leaves together and *made* themselves coverings. (Genesis 3:7)

Yatsar

In the Genesis 2 "summary" of creation that particularly speaks of the personal involvement of the Creator with man—probably written by Adam (see Genesis 5:1)—the word used for this rendering of creation is the Hebrew word *yatsar*, which means to form, fashion, shape, or sculpt. It is used only three times in the book of Genesis and only in chapter 2.

…of man:

> And the LORD God *formed* man of the dust of the ground, and breathed into his nostrils the breath of life; and man became a living being. The LORD God planted a garden eastward in Eden, and there He put the man whom He had *formed*. (Genesis 2:7-8)

…of animals:

> Out of the ground the LORD God *formed* every beast of the field and every bird of the air, and brought them to Adam to see what he would call them. And whatever Adam called each living creature, that was its name. (Genesis 2:19)

Often in the Scriptures, *yatsar* is used to describe the work necessary to make earthen pottery, as well as other personally developed materials or even plans. The context in Genesis 2 notes that when God "created" and "made" (*bārā'* and *'asah*, Genesis 1:27) the living being called "man," He "formed" (*yatsar*, Genesis 2:7) his physical frame "of the dust of the ground." Another reference to this event is found in Psalm 94:9: "He who planted the ear, shall He not hear? He who *formed* the eye, shall He not see?"

Perhaps it might be easier to understand the implications of these introductory actions if we were to evaluate them in the light of our common usage of those ideas. We often say that we have "created" something—a sculpture, a painting, a song, a book. But in reality, we have only reorganized and reshaped either matter or information that was already in existence and available.

Only God can actually "create" something that did not exist before. That is precisely how the Bible consistently uses the verb *bārā'*.

We do, however, "make" things. The best examples of our understanding of this term would be the functions of an engineer or a construction contractor. Each of those professions uses talents and training to "make" specific products from existing materials. Some of those products are large and complex (dams or bridges; houses or skyscrapers), some are intricate and mysterious (computer chips; vast Internet networks). Each, however, is "made" from existing material, however complex the assembly or different in consistency.

We can make information, too. Obviously, this involves our intellect, but we use "existing" information (either already assembled in a textbook or educational institution) to "make" additional applications or improve existing processes. Much or our modern world functions on a rather "invisible" system of knowledge stored in the computer systems of our homes and businesses. We access that information and use, reuse, apply, change, add to, rearrange, augment—in order to "make" something happen.

God took the dark, formless, empty, and shapeless "stuff" that He created *ex nihilo* (out of nothing that pre-existed) and "made" several organizational and structural changes in a sequence of dark-light cycles that were initiated rather quickly.

The final action term, *yatsar*, is more personal than merely "making." *Yatsar* implies a "hands on" involvement like "sculpting" or "painting" or "singing"—something more intimate, more emotive than just "doing." The clearest example of the Creator's personal involvement is in His "forming" the body of Adam: "And the LORD God formed man of the dust of the ground, and breathed into his nostrils the breath of life; and man became a living being" (Genesis 2:7). God was personally involved in the creation—and remains personally involved in our lives.

Understanding these three verbs gives us crucial insight into "the beginning."

Three Key Nouns

The triune nature of the Creator is an important parallel to the triune nature of the universe. The elemental structure of the universe is given to us in the initial "creation" verse. Three key nouns are used throughout the Old Testament and provide insight into the triune makeup of our universe: Time, Space, and Matter.

Bereshith

"In the beginning...." Nothing can be clearer than this phrase opening the pages of the Bible. Before this "beginning," there was nothing in existence apart from the One who caused all things to exist. Time, space, and matter first come into being here. God was the First Cause of all things. The Hebrew word is *bereshith*. It means beginning, first, best, or chief in time, place, order, or rank (i.e., time). The context will not allow a manipulation of the text by translating it "when God began to create" or by other awkward renderings.

Shamayim

The word "heavens" is from an unused Hebrew singular noun (*shaw-meh*) and is the plural form (*sha-meh* + the "*im*" ending) from that unused root. It carries the basic meaning "to be lofty" (i.e., space). That plural form (*shamayim*) is used some 420 times in the Old Testament. It can be associated with either a plural or singular verb. The heavens in this verse are not the same "heavens" created on Day Four. God doesn't mix up the order of creation. This reference in 1:1 indicates what we would understand as "space," in the sense of space-matter-time. God began with a broad stroke of creation, creating (*bārā*) from nothing the basic components of the universe as the building blocks for the rest of His creative activities.

Eretz

God also created "the earth" on Day One. The Hebrew word is *eretz* and can mean "dirt" or "dust" or a territory on earth, as in the "land of Israel"—or even earth as the planet. *Eretz* is from an unused

Hebrew root probably meaning to be firm (i.e., matter or hard-stuff). In Genesis 1:1, *eretz* refers to the material of the universe that would be organized into the fully-developed world on the subsequent days of creation.

This is essentially the "stuff" of creation. When it was created, the earth was formless (shapeless) and empty; enmeshed in a watery matrix, all of which was enclosed in dark heavens. Once this space-matter-time triune relationship was created, "making" could begin.

The Construction of the Universe Begins

> In the beginning God created the heavens and the earth. The earth was without form, and void; and darkness was on the face of the deep. And the Spirit of God was hovering over the face of the waters. (Genesis 1:1-2)

The first Hebrew word in Genesis 1:2 is the Hebrew *waw*. Every verse in Genesis 1 (except 1:1) begins with *waw*, indicating a succession of events or stages in the creation of the world. Typically, *waw* is translated "and" or "then." The consistent use of *waw* is a powerful linguistic evidence that chapter 1 is a sequential record of what God did, step by step, day by day.

Obviously, however, when the universe began, no human intelligence was there. It is interesting to note that in God's own argument for His sovereignty over humanity, He challenged the ancient man Job with several rhetorical questions, including this one:

> Where were you when I laid the foundations of the earth? Tell Me, if you have understanding. Who determined its measurements? Surely you know! Or who stretched the line upon it? To what were its foundations fastened? Or who laid its cornerstone, when the morning stars sang together, and all the sons of God shouted for joy? (Job 38:4-7)

Clearly, God is referring to the time of creation, and to the specific time He "laid the foundations of the earth," which could refer to the first day of creation, when God was involved in creating the basic components of the world. Measuring it, lining it up, fastening it, laying a cornerstone. It could also speak of Day Three, when God established the land of the earth, which would indicate the angels were created prior to Day Three. Either way, all of this speaks of the very early stages of "the heavens and the earth."

The universe is energized

Once God created "the heavens and the earth," His next step was to start the processes that make the universe function—energy, gravity, etc. He did this through the third Person of the Trinity, the Holy Spirit. The work of the Holy Spirit in creation on Day One was to energize the earth in order to prepare it for the rest of the creation events. The text states that the Spirit was "hovering," moving over the presence of the waters. This word (Hebrew *rachaph*) is used only two other times in the Old Testament (Jeremiah 23:9; Deuteronomy 32:11) and can easily be understood as "vibrating" or "fluttering."

Whatever was being done involved the very personal touch of the omnipotent and omniscient Creator. That "power" (energy) was later displayed by Jesus Christ in the seven great miracles of creation He demonstrated in public during his earthly life (recorded in the Gospel of John). Everything was prepared now for God to begin creating the various components of the world. God, the Source of all energy, powered-up the world and began to create a beautiful world in which He would place His special creation.

God prepares the cosmos for habitation

Genesis 1:1-2 contains only the first part of Day One in creation. Of course, what God did in those two verses was foundational to the rest of His creative activities.

> Then God said, "Let there be light"; and there was light. And God saw the light, that it was good; and God divided the light from the darkness. God called the light Day, and the darkness He called Night. So the evening and the

morning were the first day. (Genesis 1:3-5)

The light shines in the darkness

It has already been noted that creation involved all three members of the Godhead. In verse 3 is the first instance of God speaking: "And God said...." The Logos (the Word) of God, who is none other than the second Person of the Godhead—the One whom we identify as Jesus the Christ (John 1:1-14; Colossians 1:16-17; Hebrews 1:1-3)—participates in and begins to "call into existence" the particular details of the world.

The Father is the source of all things (v. 1), the Spirit is the energizer of all things (v. 2), and the Word is the revealer of all things (v. 3). Thus, the Word of God—who is the Light of the world—"revealed" light for the first time. Once light appeared in the world, darkness was immediately dispelled.

However, the biblical record insists that God separated the light from the darkness. This most likely indicates that the earth on Day One was in the shape of a sphere as we know it today. The words that follow confirm this fact, for God concludes Day One with "...the evening and the morning were the first day." A definite system of time had been developed, a dark-light cycle, which man observes today in the rotation of the earth, allowing light during the "morning" and darkness during the "evening."

It is worth noting that at the very "beginning," God used a specific linguistic structure to define what He was doing. There was a "light" portion, which God named "day," and a "dark" portion, which God named "night." This sequence of "evening and morning" was specifically called the first day (Genesis 1:5). That same linguistic formula is repeated throughout the following sequence of night-day cycles, reinforcing both the specificity of the phenomena and the time-motion regularity of the process.

Like clay under a seal

"Have you commanded the morning since your days began, and caused the dawn to know its place, that it might take hold of the ends of the earth, And the wicked be shaken out of it? It takes on form like clay under a seal, and stands out like a garment." (Job 38:12-14)

One of the greater mysteries of our planet is its steady rotation. Just about everything we depend on rests on the assurance that everything is basically stable. It is so dependable, in fact, that we simply expect the sun to "rise" in the morning and to "set" at night. Little thought is given to the forces involved, and especially how such phenomena came to be (scientific theories abound, of course). Long before humanity "discovered" that earth was a sphere set in the apparent nothingness of space, we were given such information by Bible writers centuries ago.

He who sits above the circle of the earth. (Isaiah 40:22)

He stretches out the north over empty space; He hangs the earth on nothing. (Job 26:7)

He prepared the heavens…He drew a circle on the face of the deep. (Proverbs 8:27)

Apparently, according to the biblical information, it was during this "first" day that the Triune Godhead shaped the watery "stuff" He had created into a "circle." That shape (probably a ball or spheroid) was "energized" by the Holy Spirit and was then set in a rotational motion. That rotation became visible when the "light" was inserted into the "heavens" and onto the "earth." Until that moment, everything was in darkness.

One other note. It also appears that this rotational energy is the source of earth's magnetic field. Modern science doesn't know for sure, since no one has been able to get down to earth's core. But it is postulated that the core of the earth is liquid, and that the lag differential between the surface rotation and the inner core motion creates a magnetic field. Humanity recognizes the effects of this field as "North" and "South" poles. The Bible simply states: "The north and the south, You have created them" (Psalm 89:12).

Good

This simple commentary repeated throughout the creation week makes a statement about the result of previous action taken each night-day cycle. This "evening and morning" that completed Day One can be summarized as follows:

- The "beginning" (time) was created

- The "heavens" (space) was created

- The "earth" (matter) was created

- The "light" (light energy) was inserted into the heavens and onto the earth

- The "north and the south" were created (rotation and magnetic field)

- The "division" of the dark and the light was established (night-day cycle)

- The entire structure of the initial cosmos was "good"

Space-Matter-Time and the Nature of God

As would be expected in any product by an intelligent being, the product (in this case the universe itself) would give some insight into the nature of the originator. The artist expresses his or her character by sculpture, painting, or musical score, or intellectual property (books, software, ideas, etc.). The architect designs buildings or bridges that display something of his or her "ideas"—which in turn are the conscious expression of that nature.

The same is true for the universe.

> The heavens declare the glory of God; And the firmament shows His handiwork. Day unto day utters speech, and night unto night reveals knowledge. There is no speech nor language where their voice is not heard. Their line has gone out through all the earth, and their words to the end of the world (Psalm 19:1-4)

> For since the creation of the world His invisible attributes are clearly seen, being understood by the things that are made, even His eternal power and Godhead (Romans 1:20)

According to the Bible, God imprinted something about Himself in the things that He created and made, so that all of humanity would be able to "clearly see" enough about God's "power and Godhead" that no one could claim ignorance or lack of exposure to the existence of a Creator-God. Those who insist on ignoring that information (the information in the creation itself) are said to be "without excuse."

In the attempt to understand the nature of the universe, theorists must often admit to reaching a possible dead end—a question that may never be satisfactorily answered. Genesis 1:1 is a satisfactory answer, but atheistic physicists and astronomers feel they must find an answer that does not involve God. It is easy to understand the motivation of atheists, but it is more difficult to understand why evangelical leaders, who insist that they hold to the inerrancy and authority of Scripture, would also insist that God would use a so-called Big Bang and vast geological ages to create, refusing to take His account of creation literally.

The tri-universe

The biblical concept of the Trinity is very difficult to understand. Theologians have argued over the practical issues of God's nature (Acts 17:29; Romans 1:20; Colossians 2:9). Many physical illustrations have been offered (an egg, the three states of matter, a triangle, etc.), but all of these are triads, not trinities. A *triad* is composed of different parts, collected together to make a different whole, but easily separated into its individual parts. A triad can also be seen as a phased sequence (e.g., liquid, gas, solid), which, although the same material, can only exist in one form at a time.

A *trinity* is both co-existent and co-terminus. That is, although composed of three different things, it cannot be separated or disconnected in any way from each "piece" of the whole.

50

Thus, the more precise illustration of God's triune nature is the universe that God Himself created. It is a "uni-verse" (one thing, containing separately definable and distinguishable entities) that cannot be taken apart. One can distinguish the different elements, and can define and describe the different functions of those elements, but can never conceive of a way to take them apart.

Space

Space itself is a trinity. Space is that in which all else exists. It is invisible, unknowable, and omnipresent. We can conceive of it as height, depth, and length, but we cannot capture or eliminate it in any way. Space is not "nothing," but whatever it is, we are unable to discover it fully. Space exists *in* all things—and all things have their existence in space. Nothing exists outside of space, except the Creator Himself and that which is created to transcend the creation by the Creator's design (e.g., angelic beings?).

The Bible word "heavens" is often used of both the atmospheric heavens (that birds fly in, for instance) and the stellar heavens (where the stars and galaxies reside). All human language uses essentially the same term for both applications, recognizing that whatever "space" is, everything that exists, exists within it and occupies it. Whatever exists cannot be taken out of space, nor can space be taken out of whatever exists.

Matter

Matter is also a trinity. Matter (mass-energy) reveals space to us and makes things visible. We see matter as a person, place, or thing and tend to define matter in terms of what we see (e.g., trees, rocks, animals, people, bacteria, stars, etc.).

As scientists learn more about the nature of matter (mass-energy), they have discovered that everything is a phenomenon of unique energy in motion, patterns and structure (e.g., molecules), and processes (e.g., motion, metabolism, etc.). Each "thing" is unique, yet exists within space, and cannot be taken out of space.

Essentially, invisible space is understood by the presence of matter in it.

We can "see" space whenever two or more organizational structures are visible. Without the visible "matter," our brain would be unable to process the "idea" of space. Humanity needs visible molecular structures in order for us to think about the invisible distances between the "pieces" of the "stuff" of creation.

Our modern telescopes have enabled us to visualize something of the immensity of space outward (the galaxies, etc.). Our microscopes have opened up a vast world of "small" things—that until very recently humanity never imagined existed. It is worth noting that the Bible writers knew about both the macro and micro aspects of creation, long before we "discovered" such things.

God told Abraham (~2,100 B.C.) that the stars of the universe were roughly equivalent to the sand grains in the earth: "...your descendants [*shall be*] as the stars of the heaven and as the sand which is on the seashore" (Genesis 22:17). The psalmist acknowledges that God protects from "the perilous pestilence...that walks in darkness" (Psalm 91:3, 6) and that his development in the womb of his earthly mother was "skillfully wrought" by God (Psalm 139:15).

While these references are surely poetic and not technical, they are nonetheless scientifically correct. In fact, modern science did not even "think" about microbes being responsible for "pestilence" until the late 1600s—and the design information responsible for life forms (the DNA) is still a jaw-dropping collection of information that only recently is beginning to be understood.

Time

Time is the third element of the tri-unity of the universe.

Man tends to view time backwards. That is, we "remember" the past, "live" in the present, and "expect" the future. Our world thinks in terms of time beginning at some definite point, then flowing through the present, and ultimately into the future. Certainly that is the way

God presents time to us "in the beginning," and we are told to "look for" the consummation of all things when God will re-create the "new heavens and new earth" in the future. Yet, time is a "created" thing, having its source in the eternal Godhead.

Time "flows" from the Creator to the universe and passes into the "historical" events of the past. We cannot understand or control time. We can only experience it. All things that exist are "experienced" through and by time. Space itself is experienced in time. Matter is only revealed as the motion that its energy manifests during time. Time cannot be separated or removed from any of the universe.

The Triune God

The opening message to humanity provides God's written revelation to man. Those words tell us how our space/matter/time universe came to exist. No other religious writings, ancient or modern, do this. All others begin with the assumption of an eternal, self-existing universe.

The Hebrew for "God" is *Elohim*, a plural noun (as noted by the "im" ending), yet normally represented by a singular pronoun "He." This is the first foreshadowing of the marvelous doctrine of the Trinity—only one Creator God, yet functioning as three divine Persons. It is significant that His created universe is actually a tri-universe, with each of its distinct components ("beginning" = time; "heaven" = space; "earth" = matter) comprising and pervading the whole universe.

Just as the Father is the source and background of all being, so space is the background of all that happens in the physical universe. Just as the Son manifests and speaks for the Father, so matter manifests and functions in space. Just as the Spirit interprets and energizes the Son and the Father in human experience, so space and matter are interpreted and experienced in phenomena operating in time.

The Father planned the work of creation, the Son did the work ("all things were made by Him"—John 1:3), and the Spirit energized it ("the Spirit of God moved"). The Triune God created and now sustains our tri-universe!

God the Father is like the space of the universe; the Source and Background of all things. God the Son is like the matter (mass-energy) of the universe; the Visible One and Revealer of the Godhead. God the Spirit is like the time of the universe; the One who makes it possible to experience the work and will of God.

Perhaps a chart will help visualize the relationship more easily.

The Father	The Son	The Holy Spirit
Is like SPACE	Is like MATTER	Is like TIME
Invisible	Visible	Sensed and Felt
Omnipresent	Tangible	Understood
Source	Present Reality	Future
God Framed	God Manifested	God Experienced
Authority	Declaration	Appropriation

An Important Application

Just as the very creation itself reflects the nature of its Creator, so is the "gospel" communicated to us.

God the Father authorizes and draws us

> For God so loved the world that He gave His only begotten Son, that whoever believes in Him should not perish but have everlasting life. For God did not send His Son into the world to condemn the world, but that the world through Him might be saved. (John 3:16-17)

> "No one can come to Me unless the Father who sent Me draws him; and I will raise him up at the last day." (John 6:44)

God the Son reveals the Father and performs the will of the Father

In the beginning was the Word, and the Word was with God, and the Word was God. He was in the beginning with God. All things were made through Him, and without Him nothing was made that was made....And the Word became flesh and dwelt among us, and we beheld His glory, the glory as of the only begotten of the Father, full of grace and truth. (John 1:1-3, 14)

Jesus said to him, "...He who has seen Me has seen the Father; so how can you say, 'Show us the Father'?" (John 14:9)

"For I have come down from heaven, not to do My own will, but the will of Him who sent Me." (John 6:38)

Yet it pleased the LORD to bruise Him; He has put Him to grief. When You make His soul an offering for sin... (Isaiah 53:10)

Jesus spoke these words and said: "Father, the hour has come....You have given Him authority over all flesh, that He should give eternal life to as many as You have given Him. And this is eternal life, that they may know You, the only true God, and Jesus Christ whom You have sent. I have glorified You on the earth. I have finished the work which You have given Me to do." (John 17:1-4)

Moreover, brethren, I declare to you the gospel....that Christ died for our sins according to the Scriptures, and that He was buried, and that He rose again the third day according to the Scriptures. (1 Corinthians 15:1-4)

God the Spirit brings the experience of the Godhead to us

"But the Helper, the Holy Spirit, whom the Father will send in My name, He will teach you all things, and bring to your remembrance all things that I said to you." (John 14:16)

"Nevertheless I tell you the truth. It is to your advantage that I go away; for if I do not go away, the Helper will not come to you; but if I depart, I will send Him to you. And when He has come, He will convict the world of sin, and of righteousness, and of judgment." (John 16:7-8)

...do you not know that your body is the temple of the Holy Spirit who is in you, whom you have from God, and you are not your own? (1 Corinthians 16:19)

...having believed, you were sealed with the Holy Spirit of promise, who is the guarantee of our inheritance until the redemption of the purchased possession, to the praise of His glory. (Ephesians 1:13-14)

God "creates" us when we are twice-born

Therefore, if anyone is in Christ, he is a new creation; old things have passed away; behold, all things have become new. (2 Corinthians 5:17)

...the new man which was created according to God, in true righteousness and holiness. (Ephesians 4:24)

CHAPTER THREE
THE BEGINNING OF THE EARTH

Once the initial universe is created by the will and purpose of God (Revelation 4:11), the Triune Godhead now "makes" and "shapes" the earth (*eretz*) and the heavens (*shamayim*) into an organized and functioning *cosmos* in preparation for the life that would be created on Days Five and Six. The crowning "image of God" would be charged with the responsibility of caring for the creation.

The first two verses of Genesis only summarize what was done on the first "evening and morning." It should be noted that the first day was an enormous event.

- The "beginning" (time) was created

- The "heavens" (space) was created

- The "earth" (matter) was created

- The "light" (light energy) was inserted into the heavens and onto the earth

- The "north and the south" were created (rotation and magnetic field)

- The "division" of the dark and the light was established (night-day cycle)

• The entire structure of the initial cosmos was "good"

The Dating of the Universe

As was noted previously, the evolutionary naturalist would insist that the universe is somewhere between 18 and 20 billions of years old. That is, *if* there was a beginning to the universe instead of an eternal cycle of expansion and contraction of all mass-energy. More modern scientists would follow the idea that there was an explosion (the Big Bang) of a microscopic speck that contained all mass-energy—somehow coming into existence by itself microseconds before it exploded. Obviously, none of this has been observed by any human being, but belief in the idea is strong.

The earth was to have "formed" some 4.5 billion years ago after the stars and galaxies coalesced out of the energy and gases disbursed from the Big Bang.

Those ideas, of course, are nowhere alluded to in the Bible—anywhere.

Hybrid Theories

What is troubling, however, is that many evangelical theologians and scientists seem to embrace the idea that "science" has proven that the universe *is* very old. The biblical information must, therefore, accommodate the "proof" of those billions of years. There are several of these "hybrid" theories, each of them promoted by a sizeable numbers of evangelical scholars who embrace the necessity of deep time to explain the "good" of geology and vast distances of galaxies.

Theistic Evolution

The teachers of Theistic Evolution believe that "creation" occurred *by means of* "evolution." The only practical difference between this theory and the atheistic presumptions of the naturalist is merely that "God" uses evolution. Most of the mainline Christian schools and universities espouse Theistic Evolution. Secular schools, colleges, and universities teach only naturalism and strongly exclude any idea of the supernatural. Some who embrace the overall idea of Theistic Evolution will allow for a "providential" involvement in the overall scheme of the process, but all of the evolutionary processes are presumed to be the mechanism by which God brought the universe, earth, and life into existence. Like the Deist, God is distant, disinterested, and disconnected from our reality.

The Bible, we are told, may "contain" the message of God, but the concept of an inerrant and inspired written text from God is not accepted. The book of Genesis, especially, is considered to be a collection of myths or legends, similar to the many mythologies of ancient Babylon, Greece, and other pagan religions.

Thus, all those who believe in Theistic Evolution would date the creation of the universe by evolutionary ideas—between 18 and 20 billion years ago.

The Day-Age Theory

The major difference between the Day-Age Theory and Theistic Evolution is that there is an attempt to follow the biblical sequence of the seven days outlined in Genesis 1. That is, each "day" represents a series of developments, overseen by God, wherein the "creative" acts are intermingled with naturalistic processes. Some would suggest that God's intervention is more evident during the development of life, but the biblical information is merely an allegory meant to teach us that God exists and was, somehow, involved in the early origins.

"Day One" could represent the earliest eons of the expansion and coalescing of dust and gases as they stretched out after the Big Bang. "Day Two" might be the way God expressed the formation of the early earth's sphere and the organizational separation of the early elements, etc. Days Three, Four, Five, and Six each demonstrate the continued development of the universe, with a special emphasis on the earth.

God is "active" in a passive sort of way, and He "monitors" and "insures" that everything will be "good" in the end. There are some very obvious disagreements with the evolutionary model of progression and the biblical text, however.

The Theistic Evolutionists do not attempt to equate the language of the Bible with their theory—even though most of them would insist that they believe in a "real" God. The Day-Age proponents, in contrast, try to draw direct analogies between the information about each "day" as recorded in Genesis. Once again, the old age of the evolutionary requirements are embraced, as well as the procedural development of the evolutionary model. Thus, the universe "began" between 18 and 20 billion years ago, and earth became an identifiable planet around 4.5 billion years ago.

Progressive Creation

While similar to the Day-Age Theory, the various modifications of Progressive Creation attempt to be more biblical, and therefore, more acceptable to evangelical theologians, scholars, and pastors. Essentially, those who promote the idea of progressive creation would insist that God was directly involved in several specific stages of creation throughout the long ages. For instance, God created the energy speck that exploded in the Big Bang (or the Big Bang is the result of God's initial creation).

But God then allowed the natural forces to develop over the course of eons of time until certain divine creative events were required. There are many variations on this, of course, but all Progressive Creationists appear to agree that God had to "create" first life. Several other "events" were necessary for God to intervene. Some suggest that the huge change from non-living chemicals to single-cell life and the development of marine invertebrates would require God's creative power. Other events like the transition from fish to amphibians, various interventions or guidance for reptiles, mammals, hominids—and finally man are considered "creative" acts.

Many Progressive Creationists would believe that Adam and Eve were "real" historical humans, created uniquely by God somewhere around 10,000 years ago. Others within Progressive Creation (mainly within the broad Intelligent Design Movement) would not be as firm about the special nature of man, but that somewhere recently, soulless hominids developed into what we now classify as *Homo sapiens*, and a pair (Adam and Eve) were singled out to receive God's special attention.

Obviously, Progressive Creation theorists vary widely. The common denominators appear to be that development (evolutionary processes) is "natural" and that God uses the "natural" laws that science has uncovered as His design. All proponents would insist that physical death is an integral part of the universe from the earliest functioning of replicating "life." Those who would incorporate a biblical background for their model are the more conservative and thus more often embraced by the evangelical movement.

However, all who embrace the concept of Progressive Creation hold to an "old earth" viewpoint, and thus endorse the 18 to 20 billion-year-old universe and a 4.5 billion-year-old earth.

The Gap Theory

In the past, the most widely accepted hybrid theory among conservative churches was the dispensational teaching that there had been an earlier "world" that was destroyed when Lucifer fell from heaven in his rebellion against the Creator. That "pre-adamic" age lasted for an unknown number of eons, but accounts for the alleged billions of years prior to the re-creation after Satan's fall. A "gap" was thus inserted between the first two verses of Genesis 1.

> In the beginning God created the heavens and the earth. *[Implied Gap]* The earth was without form, and void; and darkness was on the face of the deep. And the Spirit of God was hovering over the face of the waters. (Genesis 1:1-2)

In the text, the earth is described as "without form" and "void." Proponents of the Gap Theory usually translate these words as "ruined" and "desolate," indicating something bad had happened previously. In essence, the theory suggests that God did indeed create the heavens and the earth, but a cataclysmic event occurred after the initial creation, demanding the judgment of God, and thus ruining the earth and leaving it desolate. The terms are, however, more commonly understood in the Bible as "formless" and "empty" or "uninhabited."

The apparent reading of the text would be that God created the heavens and the earth in their basic elemental components (space and matter), and these were without form and empty, waiting to be developed by God. Some among those who still retain a belief in the Gap Theory teach that there was a race of pre-adamic men, similar to the "giants" mentioned in Genesis chapter 6. While this version of the Gap Theory is somewhat controversial, the common teaching among all proponents is that an "older" world grew more and more evil over time, and was ultimately destroyed.

Made popular by the Scofield Bible of the early 1900s, this "ruin and reconstruction" idea is alleged to be further verified by the fossil record. The various gigantic fossils (dinosaurs, etc.) are assumed to be additional evidence of a pre-adamic time that lasted for eons under the rule of Satan. Some suggest that since there are few verified human fossils, the "race" that inhabited earth back then was some sort of "hybrid" of mammals and demons. Some would even suggest that the so-called "cave men" (hominid fossils) relate to that pre-adamic time.

This "gap" between Genesis 1:1 and 1:2 is not linguistically, grammatically, or doctrinally *required* in any sense. It doesn't even hold up to basic logic. A cataclysm sufficiently powerful to leave the earth "without form and void" would destroy any physical evidence of that event (like fossils), and would do away with the intended place for the billions of years to accrue. Furthermore, God's ultimate pronouncement of "good" on "everything that he had made" (Genesis 1:31) would be meaningless if there had been ages of wickedness prior to God's final evaluation of His work. Obviously, no evolutionist accepts the Gap Theory.

Common problems among the hybrids

All of these various hybrids (except the Gap Theory) require that naturalistic evolution be a "normal" part of how God involves Himself in the creation process. The only practical reason to accept long ages is to allow for an evolutionary scheme to "fit" into the Bible, since the philosophical foundation of evolutionary theory is "deep time"—billions of years. The rationale for evolutionary development over time, however, is "natural selection." Something (besides time) must provide an intellectual basis for the upward movement (simple to complex). Natural selection is that rationale.

Dr. Stephen Jay Gould, one of the most prominent of 20th century evolutionists, had this to say about the necessary "natural selection" component of all evolutionary processes.

> Moreover, natural selection, expressed in inappropriate human terms, is a remarkably inefficient, even cruel process. Selection carves adaptation by eliminating masses of the less fit—imposing hecatombs of death as preconditions for limited increments of change. Natural selection is a theory of "trial and error externalism"—organisms propose via their storehouse of variation, and environments dispose of nearly all—not an efficient and human "goal-directed internalism" (which would be fast and lovely, but nature does not know the way).[1]

Evolution, if used by God in any form, charges the Creator with waste and cruelty. God must be either ignorant or impotent, since He must experiment and use trial and error to bring about the "most fit." Also, over the long ages of "natural" development, God would have to consciously choose the most inefficient, cruel, and wasteful process to create. Those factors would make death the device of God to produce this "best" over time. Death becomes "good," when the Bible calls it the last enemy to be defeated.

These various attempts to harmonize the text of Scripture with the "proofs" of modern science necessitate that God is the "Evolver" (Theistic Evolution), or the "Guide or Experimenter" (Day-Age and

---

1   Stephen Jay Gould, 1994, The Power of This View of Life, *Natural History*, 103: 6.

Progressive Creation), or the "Reconstructionist" (the Gap Theory). Each of these hybrids require that one must either reject the text (Theistic Evolution), allegorize the text (Day-Age), deconstruct the words of the text (Progressive Creation), or insert a "catch-all" theory into the clear reading of the text (the Gap Theory).

All of these hybrid theories are attempts to accommodate the ages of evolutionary development. Each of them, in one way or another, makes God the author of some 4.5 billion years of death and confusion.

However, Romans 5:12 insists that death is the result of sin, and this fact is either openly ignored or reinterpreted by these hybrids. 1 Corinthians 14:33 clearly states that God does not author confusion, but confusion and random processes lie at the very core of the evolutionary theory. All of these various accommodations to evolutionary naturalism fly in the face of biblical revelation and the attributes of God.

Exodus 20:11 states the reason for the fourth commandment (God worked six days and rested one day). Those words, *inscribed twice* with the finger of God, cannot be taken in any sense as "ages" during which we are to "work" and "rest." We, who are His created stewards, are to follow His example.

From a biblical perspective, all hybrid theories of creation are severely lacking.

When Then?

When considering the age of the earth, the main point of *agreement* between the creationist and the evolutionist is that recorded human history began only a few thousand years ago. Before that time one can only speculate about what happened—or, as in the case of the biblical creationist, refer to what has been given through divine revelation.

Many scholars have tried hard to produce a complete chronology of the Bible, especially the date of creation. Just about all of them disagree in some point or another, demonstrating the difficulty of the task. That task is compounded when additional information is considered and compared to the biblical data.

- The Masoretic, Sepuagint, and Samaritan texts of the Old Testament all differ in their chronology of the ancient histories of man.

- There is disagreement among biblical scholars about the length of the calendar year prior to our more modern calculations.

- There appear to be missing generations among the lists in the biblical text—especially in Genesis 11.

- There are confusing and apparently contradictory records of the kings of Israel and Judah—even more challenging when compared to the secular chronologies of Egypt and Babylon.

- The various physical methods of dating the earth vary widely both in methodology and in result, adding more confusion to the search for an accurate chronology.

If one believes that the Bible is both inspired and inerrant, even a very cursory reading of Scripture would reveal this clear framework:

- Genesis 1 describes the time from the initial creation of the universe to the creation of man.

- Genesis 5 gives chronological information that specifies the time from Adam and Eve to the great Flood of Noah's day.

- Genesis 11 connects the timeline from the end of the great Flood to the time of Abraham. The date of Abraham's birth has broad agreement among both secular and Bible historians.

- The Old Testament historical books (Genesis, Exodus, Numbers, Joshua, Judges, 1 and 2 Samuel, 1 and 2 Kings, and 1 and 2 Chronicles) deliver a running record of the nation of Israel from Abraham to the nation's captivity under Nebuchadnezzar.

- Several of the prophetic books (Isaiah, Jeremiah, Daniel) and the post-captivity historical books (Ezra and Nehemiah) make available the timeline for the captivity of Israel to her restoration as a nation.

- From the close of the prophetic books (Malachi) to the beginning of the time of Christ, secular histories provide the record of events which tie the 400-year silence of the biblical books to the historical event of the birth of Jesus of Nazareth.

Even with a strong belief in the accuracy of Scripture, those who hold to a biblically revealed chronology still vary. Jewish calendars list the creation event as happening during 3760 B.C. Archbishop Ussher (probably the most famous and scholarly of the chronologists) gives 4004 B.C. as the date. Others whose names are well known (Josephus, Luther, Kepler, etc.) are two to three thousand years apart. More recent Bible historians give dates from 6,000 to 40,000 B.C. All of this demonstrates that it is difficult to "prove" a given date for the birth of the planet.

However, it should be noted that none of these careful Bible historians allow for anything like "millions" let alone "billions" of years. That's why there is not much wiggle room for positioning in the age arguments: one either accepts the "young earth" or the "old earth," but not a "middle-age" earth. It really isn't possible to have it both ways.

Just so that the view of this author is clear, the weight of the biblical data favors the more recent dates, not the expanded dates. The earth is certainly less than 10,000 years old and probably closer to 6,000 years old. (More on this in Chapter 9.)

The Second Day

Since all actual written historical records agree substantially with the biblical record, there is no reason not to accept the Bible's information—except for personal preference. With the assurance that the Bible presents the creation of the universe (Day One) as recent as 6,000 years ago, the shaping of the earth occurs 24 hours after that initial creation event.

> Then God said, "Let there be a firmament in the midst of the waters, and let it divide the waters from the waters." Thus God made the firmament, and divided the waters which were under the firmament from the waters which were above the firmament; and it was so. And God called the firmament Heaven. So the evening and the morning were the second day. (Genesis 1:6-8)

The firmament

Day Two of creation involved the making (*'asah*) of the "firmament" and the "dividing" of the waters. The British translators choice of "firmament" comes from the Hebrew *raqiya* and is usually translated "expanse" in more recent Bible versions. The Hebrew term clearly means an "extended surface" or a "thin, stretched-out space." This *raqiya* is inserted in the "waters," causing them to be "divided." Some of these "waters" were to be situated above the *raqiya*, and the remainder were to stay below. Peter speaks of "the earth standing out of water and in the water" (2 Peter 3:5), and the prophet Isaiah tells us that as God sat above the circle of the earth, He "stretches out the heavens like a curtain, and spreads them out like a tent to dwell in" (Isaiah 40:22).

The Hebrew word *raqiya* is only used 17 times in the entire Old Testament, and is often used to describe different "expanses." The "speech" and "knowledge" of the Creator are openly declared in the "firmament" (Psalm 19:1-2)—indeed the very "invisible" power and divine nature are "clearly seen" by the created work of God (Romans 1:20). The startling vision of Ezekiel describes a "firmament" above the heads of the "Cherubim" that was like a "sapphire" supporting the throne of God (Ezekiel 1:26 and 10:1). Daniel tells us that the "wise" will shine like the "brightness of the firmament" and the "stars"

(Daniel 12:3). Obviously, the Hebrew term is meant to be descriptive rather than nominative. *Raqiya* is a "thing" that God made, but it is more often used as an adjective to describe how it is used. Perhaps that is why God specifically named the *raqiya* "heaven" (Genesis 1:8).

While the specific naming of the "expanse" is designated as "heaven" during the activity of the second day, the Old Testament uses the proper name ("heaven") over 400 times, and in several different ways.

- It is used of both the solar system and the starry universe as God describes the "lights" that He develops on the fourth day (Genesis 1:14-17). This broad and inclusive use is common (both to us in normal speech and in the language of the Old Testament).

- It is used of the atmosphere in which the birds are to fly "above the earth across the face of the firmament of the heavens" (Genesis 1:20). The birds "of the air" are mentioned an additional 16 times in the Old Testament.

- It is used by God Himself during His discourse with Job to describe the stars and galaxies of the universe: "Can you bind the cluster of the Pleiades, Or loose the belt of Orion? Can you bring out Mazzaroth in its season? Or can you guide the Great Bear with its cubs?" (Job 38:31-32).

- It is also used specifically of the sun and moon (our near solar system). "Then Joshua spoke to the LORD…Sun, stand still over Gibeon; And Moon, in the Valley of Aijalon….So the sun stood still in the midst of heaven" (Joshua 10:12-13).

Whatever was done on the second day was significant enough for God to take a full "work day" to accomplish it. Later, the Holy Spirit inspired Peter to record that the "waters above" were totally destroyed at the time of the great Flood during Noah's time (2 Peter 3:5-6).

You alone are the LORD; You have made heaven, The heaven of heavens, with all their host, The earth and everything on it, The seas and all that is in them, And You preserve them all. The host of heaven worships You. (Nehemiah 9:6)

The waters above

Whatever physical properties may have been described by the information that God provides about the second day, it is clear the upper "waters" would have been invisible to earth inhabitants. The sun, moon, and stars would later become time references that would necessitate visibility from earth's surface. Those "waters" that remained below would eventually become "seas" on the earth's surface. In between, in the *raqiya*, all the elements necessary to sustain the "breath of life" would be formed and maintained.

What kind of water would God have placed above this expanse? Whatever it was, it would not have consisted of clouds or mist or fog; these all have droplets of water that obscure light. Nor could it have been some form of ice band in the upper reaches of the earth's "heaven," since such a barrier would either obscure the sun or be melted by it. Some have suggested that the "waters" were diffused to the outer rim of the universe itself, thus placing them beyond the sun, moon, and stars. Still others have postulated that the upper "waters" were dispersed through space in some form of "dark matter."

In addition, there is an implication that the hydrological cycle as we know it today (rain, evaporation, rain), was not functioning then, but some sort of "mist" system watered the ground (Genesis 2:5-6). If those biblical hints are to be taken at face value, then the most likely explanation seems to be a spherical band of "waters" surrounding the earth's atmosphere. A blanket of water vapor in the ionosphere, for instance, would be quite invisible and not obstruct the light of the heavenly bodies.

Obviously, none of us really knows. We are faced with the biblical information that this first cosmos was "standing out of water and in the water" and that unique condition "perished" under the awful cataclysm of the global Flood (2 Peter 3:5-6). That biblical scenario is verified by all of our modern scientific observations—to the extent that there is no such "water" above anywhere now, nor could the atmospheric conditions as we now know them ever rain for "40 days and 40 nights." Either conditions were very different in the past as the Bible suggests, or the Bible is simply wrong. There is no in-between on this issue.

It does appear, however, that the earth *was* very different in the past. The fossil record provides evidence of a vastly different climate and ecological distribution than we observe today. Studies have indicated that the total biomass in the past (the total of all the carbon-based systems) was nearly 100 times greater than we can account for today. Coal accumulations are huge, indicating caches of plant material mushed and crushed together in seams spanning hundreds of miles. Antarctica contains one of the largest coal deposits in the world. There are billions of fish fossils, massed both in depth and distribution over the entire planet. Fossil graveyards (many millions of bones) are scrambled and mingled in enormous deposits. Many fossils of plants and animals are much larger than the comparative specimens alive today (ferns, trees, squids and sharks, cockroaches and dragonflies, alligators and dinosaurs, stegodons and sloths, etc.)—the list is both amazing and a bit frightening.

Earth's catastrophic past is well documented.

Just what caused that different past is not known scientifically, but the biblical model for "waters above the firmament" suggests an intellectually plausible description of an environmental structure that would be sufficient, physically, to produce both the fossil abnormalities that we know about as well as provide for the biblical information about human longevity. Whatever or however the "waters" were distributed above the earth surface, they would have produced several effects in the past that we do not observe today.

- There would have been a greenhouse effect. Wide distribution of tropical plants (ferns, palm trees, etc.) and cold-blooded animals (reptiles, etc.) would have been aided by a worldwide distribution and diffusion of the sun's energy. Today, the earth's habitable zone is quite small compared to its total surface. Something redistributed the energy/heat from the sun differently than we can observe today.

- A filtering of radioactive waves and particles from space would have been the result of a shield of "waters." If such a band were interposed between the sun and the earth—even between the solar system and the outer universe—the shield impact would have been significant.

- A reduction in air currents (and the resulting storms) would have followed some sort of water shield above the atmosphere. Such air currents are caused by temperature differences over large areas. If the earth were largely sub-tropical in the past (as appears from the fossil record), then there would have been far less cyclonic and disastrous environmental forces at work.

- There would be an absence of deserts and polar caps. Evidence abounds that the modern deserts and polar ice are "new" to the planet's history—new in the sense of very recent. Ruins of cities are well known, as well as "stories" of disappearing ecological histories. What is available to our observation today verifies that our earth was very different not so very long ago.

- The Bible records longevity of life during that first world that is not experienced today. What little we know about aging indicates that our cellular disintegration is hastened by exposure both to the radiation of the sun and the extremes of climate.

Modern physics has difficulty in modeling how any form of water band would have been constructed. There are difficulties with the weight of such a band of water above the near atmosphere, and problems with the energy distribution—both that which would be necessary to maintain it and that which would be required to keep the "waters" in a vapor form. Therefore, many creationists struggle with a scientific understanding of just what these "waters above the firmament" were.

Whatever it was, it is not here now (2 Peter 3:6).

Nonetheless, the Bible clearly insists that the "waters" were "divided" on the second day, and in so doing, the structure of the universe and the watery matrix of Day One was forever altered.

The Third Day

The second day is a day of preparation and security. Some form of expanse was positioned between the watery matrix of Day One, with the result that two major sets of "waters" were developed; one set was positioned "above" a second set "below." Whatever was done during that second day, the new structure was sufficient to provide a foundation for a cosmos that was to support vast biological processes. The evening-morning cycle continued to work and the "making" of the Third Day begins.

> Then God said, "Let the waters under the heavens be gathered together into one place, and let the dry land appear"; and it was so. And God called the dry land Earth, and the gathering together of the waters He called Seas. And God saw that it was good. (Genesis 1:9-10)

Gathering the waters together

Until the organization of both the "waters under the heavens" and the remaining *eretz* (the hard stuff) into "dry land," there is no evidence either in science or in the text of Scripture to suggest that the original nature of the stuff of creation was anything more than a "formless and empty" blob. Whatever happened on the third day began with organizational processes acting on the rotating sphere that had been set in motion on the first day and separated into a separate body of "waters" on the second day. Now, on the third day, the earth begins to take shape.

There a few side issues worth noting here.

- Gravity is still something of a mystery to science. We know that the "force" of gravity is proportional to the "mass" (size and density) of a given structure (planet, star, etc.). But we do not know *how* gravity is formed, maintained, or even what it consists of.

- Magnetic fields are *not* the same as gravity. Magnetic fields have "poles" (north and south, positive and negative); gravity is different. Magnetic fields are better understood today and seem to be related to differential movement, current through a wire, directional movements of molten rock, lag time between the earth's core and its surface rotation, etc. But we still don't *know* how these processes started.

- Circular motion tends to throw particles away from the center of the motion—unless the particles are "contained" by a barrier of some kind (think water in a bucket being whirled around by a kid in a science project).

There are some fundamental problems here. The rotation of the earth would seem to fling the material of the earth out into space. Of course, gravity is that which probably holds it together, but what happened to initialize the balance? The earth's magnetic field (which has nothing to do with gravity) seems to be dependent on the rotational motion of the earth. What keeps the earth at a constant speed? How do we begin to understand the most basic of these questions when we can only measure the effects?

One of the basic mysteries of our understanding about the nature of matter is that the various energies involved are somewhat contradictory—this is especially true at the macro level (gravity, orbits of solar system bodies, stars, galaxies, etc.). Oh, yes, theories abound, and there are many mathematical models that are used to demonstrate the current status of our thinking, but we don't *know*.

How can our planet remain suspended in space on "nothing" as described in Job (Job 26:6)? What holds the earth's "foundations" together (Psalm 104:5)? How can the incessant tides and actions of the oceans not destroy the land surfaces, and how do the continents remain in place (Jeremiah 5:22)? What keeps the star configurations so precise and regular (Job 38:31-33)? What, in fact, holds everything together, and why doesn't the universe simply explode, implode, or collapse?

Enormous energies are involved in maintaining the rotation of our earth. Gravity's unfathomable force appears to be that which keeps the earth from being torn apart by the very forces that keep "evening and morning" going. Those isolated concerns of our planet are compounded by the enormity of the intertwined complexity of the universe. Astronomers and physicists make some urbane speculations about these issues, but scientifically, there is no testable answer to these huge questions except the simple biblical answers that an omnipotent and omniscient Creator designed and made "the worlds" that way, and everything is now held together by the same authority and power that created it in the first place (Colossians 1:17; Hebrews 1:3).

In one place

We have already reviewed some of the differences between the biblical account of the creation cosmology and our ability to observe the various components of our environmental functions today. The third day involved huge organizational forces of the watery matrix, coalescing the "seas" into structured water resource systems.

> When He prepared the heavens, I was there, When He drew a circle on the face of the deep, when He established the clouds above, When He strengthened the fountains of the deep, when He assigned to the sea its limit, so that the waters would not transgress His command, when He marked out the foundations of the earth. (Proverbs 8:27-29)

> "Where were you when I laid the foundations of the earth? Tell Me, if you have understanding. Who determined its

measurements? Surely you know! Or who stretched the line upon it? To what were its foundations fastened? Or who laid its cornerstone, when the morning stars sang together, and all the sons of God shouted for joy?" (Job 38:4-7)

The biblical phrase is: "Let the waters under the heaven be gathered together into _one place_ [emphasis mine]...and the gathering together of the waters He called Seas." That condition does not exist today. The earth's oceans are spread over many places, with residues of large inland lakes and river drainage systems that bear very little resemblance to the biblical descriptions of that First Age. Not only were the waters/seas "gathered" in one place, but there were "fountains of the deep" established sometime during this process, as well as a vast water spring that was the source for four major rivers.

> Now a river went out of Eden to water the garden, and from there it parted and became four riverheads. (Genesis 2:10)

> When he established the clouds above: when he strengthened the fountains of the deep. (Proverbs 8:28)

> In the six hundredth year of Noah's life, in the second month, the seventeenth day of the month, on that day all the fountains of the great deep were broken up, and the windows of heaven were opened. (Genesis 7:11)

While these references are just pieces of the picture, they do give us some biblical insight to the structure of that first creation cosmology. The Bible, in several places, indicates that the universe and the earth that God brought into existence was quite different from what we experience now. God has revealed His long-range plan to us in 2 Peter 3. Perhaps a quick summary of those insights will help as we evaluate the third day.

The First Age	The Second Age	The Third Age
From creation to the Flood of Noah's day (2 Peter 3:5-6). That cosmos, which was destroyed by the Flood, no longer exists. We have no access to those structural aspects (waters above the waters; everything "very good;" longevity of living creatures; etc.).	From the Flood of Noah's day until utter destruction of the universe (2 Peter 3:7-9). That age (our age) is characterized by "preservation" and "longsuffering" (Colossians 1:17; Hebrews 1:3). All that we can measure and test is being "reserved" (kept, guarded) by the same "word" that brought it into existence in the first place. The operative force in nature is to conserve, not innovate.	From the utter destruction of the universe throughout eternity (2 Peter 3:10-13). This is the condition that we loosely call "heaven." The descriptions available to us in the Bible insist that this "new heavens and new earth" is absolutely different from anything that we can adequately conceive of, given our current environmental constraints.

Earth and its produce

Then God said, "Let the earth bring forth grass, the herb that yields seed, and the fruit tree that yields fruit according to its kind, whose seed is in itself, on the earth"; and it was so. And the earth brought forth grass, the herb that yields seed according to its kind, and the tree that yields fruit, whose seed is in itself according to its kind. And God saw that it was good. So the evening and the morning were the third day. (Genesis 1:11-13)

Certainly one of the more controversial discussions of our day is the theory that various biological systems develop over long ages by natural processes. The Bible seems to lump all of plant science into one day's event. Not only that, but the Bible indicates that all of the earth's plant life was in existence prior to the sun, upon which every plant on the earth's surface depends in some way. How could such be?

The narrative language of the third day uses specific Hebrew terms. After the water was "gathered together" and the "dry land" appeared, the earth was told (ordered by the Creator) to "bring forth!" Many of the modern translations use such terms as "sprout" or "produce" when converting the Hebrew phrase. The popular Bible paraphrase *The Message* renders the command: "Earth, green up!" Well, maybe that's a bit of poetic license, but the text does use command language, and the literal representation of the words would be very similar: "Then God said, 'Earth, grow (sprout, produce) grass...!'" Please remember that the Bible specifically designates all of these earth products as "food" for the living creatures that were later to populate the planet (Genesis 1:30). The text records how earth responded; we are told that the earth did indeed produce a three-fold category of its "produce."

- Grass – essentially all ground-covering vegetation
- Herbs – would apply to all bushes and shrubs
- Trees – probably includes all large woody plants

Plants are not simple

There is no hint anywhere, either in science or in the Scripture, that reproducing plants are the same as "earth" (dirt). There is a vast difference between dirt and grass, for instance, and the stunning molecular makeup of reproducing biology is logarithmically beyond the molecular simplicity of dirt and rock. The complexity of cellular structure and exceedingly sophisticated energy conversion mechanisms like photosynthesis far surpass the soil in which most of earth's "produce" lives out its cycle.

To begin with, none of the "dirt" formations reproduce. Yes, some "grow" (like crystals, stalactites, stalagmites, etc.), but they do not adapt to any environmental changes as can and do reproductive plants. Rocks don't rock—they sit still for a very long time. Plants rock! They sway to the wind, they move in relationship to the sun, they even respond to sounds and atmospheric pressure. Yes, rocks can be pretty, but plants are beautiful. The Lord Jesus said that even the most wealthy and glorious king who has ever lived was not clothed like the beauty of the "wild flowers" of the field (Luke 12:27).

After its kind

God introduces a repetitive phrase on Day Three that is used ten times in the first chapter alone, an additional seven times speaking of the animals at the time of Noah's Flood, and another 13 times in Leviticus and Deuteronomy defining the specific types of animal sacrifices and flesh that was suitable to eat.

Evidently the concept is important.

All of the plants of the third day were to have "seed" imbedded within the very nature of the plant itself, and all of the subsequent "yielding" of that seed (reproduction) was to be "according to its kind." Everything we know about the biology of plants verifies this simple statement. The biological structure and nature of any given earth "produce" is contained within the cellular information of that specific plant. That very complex internal information assures us that an apple tree will not produce kumquats, and that a rose (however broadly expressed) will never become a petunia.

> For every tree is known by its own fruit. For men do not gather figs from thorns, nor do they gather grapes from a bramble bush. (Luke 6:44)

Not everybody agrees just what the Hebrew word for "kind" (Hebrew *min*) means. The biblical use of the word *min* is mostly applied to living things: everything from grasshoppers to cattle. It probably is not limited to our biological term *species*, which is a modern classification not necessarily related to DNA distinctions. It could apply to *genus*, or perhaps to *family*, but scientific studies are complex and have not yet provided enough precision to determine with any certainty where *min* begins or stops.

However, one biological function is certain. There is absolutely no proof of a "common ancestor" to all living things—other than as told by the sophisticated stories of evolutionary naturalism. What is absolutely certain, as far as observation is concerned is that every plant and every animal reproduces only "after its kind." Each has its own DNA and can only direct the reproduction of the same "kind." There is no indication that a fish can become a duck or that algae can become a cow—none. Time is irrelevant. The informational changes are so vast, that no amount of "random mutations" could ever innovate those huge structural changes to the cellular data.

Written in the informational instructions of every reproductive "kind" are multiple "languages" for unique needs, back-up systems, timing increments, master "blueprints," and cross checks that verify the proper "connections." The more we begin to discover these genetic instructions, the more complex and "design intensive" the information becomes. *Random* and *purposelessness* are hardly the words to apply to the Creator's order "after its kind."

Furthermore, the commonly used term "natural selection" is so often personified that it has become a de facto "intelligent designer" (lower case intended). Natural selection is said to "operate on," "choose" and "favor" and "provide"—all terms associated with intelligent decisions, none of which is present in unguided nature. The very term "selection" is both deceptive on the one hand and purposely kept in the story on the other because it gives to randomness the character of an overarching deity which/who can "fulfill" the "needs" of the planet.

None of this is empirical science, of course, but rather fanciful and sophisticated storytelling. If true, the biblical account of creation can be jettisoned. What is *observed*, what is *known*, is that natural processes are at best conservative (they keep things stable) and over time, life, order, and information deterioration, these processes become extinct and die; "natural" processes do not "select" anything. Environments do not "operate on" animals.

Animals do "adapt," but that adaptation ability is "within" the reproductive "seed" of that which exists. The "kind" surely does have the information necessary within the gene pool to adapt to environmental conditions. Plant and animal breeders take advantage of this phenomenon all the time—but they use the information already available in the plant or animal (the DNA), and then the breeder—an intelligent human—"selects" the characteristics that *he* desires.

So What!

Skimming a rock over the surface of a lake is fun, but it doesn't do much except make puddles and then drop to the bottom of the lake. But if you follow the splashes, you can see a trail that leaves a lasting impression in your mind. In some sense, that's what has been done in this chapter about the second and third days of creation. There's a big "lake" of unknowns we encounter when we discuss the origins of the universe and the earth. We can pick up a "rock" from the information "beach" that we can see and experience, try to throw it across the lake to the other side, only to find that the rock just skipped over the lake—and that the lake was too big!

That's where faith comes in. Either we believe that the lake has always been here and that our personal prowess will sooner or later be sufficient to show the lake who's boss, or we will admit that the lake (and everything around it) was put there by design and on purpose. There is not much intellectual middle ground for these presuppositions—because we "wake up" on the lake! We were not here when the lake was formed. Yes, we can pick up the rock and we can throw it with all our strength onto the lake surface, but the lake just sits there, absorbs the puddles that our rock makes, and stays as it was—a lake.

There are two very different faith stories about how the lake got there.

One story begins with the assumption that there is no "Lake Creator." Therefore, everything about the lake must be described in terms of natural forces. Those of us who now live around the lake are obviously more intelligent than the lake, so we swimmers and rock throwers should feel free to embellish the legends about the "beginning" of the lake. Those stories get more technical (and fanciful) as they are told and retold, but one constant remains: There is no "instant" lake, and the answers to the questions about how the lake got here are to be found in and among the observable processes that keep the lake functioning.

The other story recognizes at the outset that the lake is much bigger and has a bigger story to "tell" than we who live around the lake could ever imagine on our own. When we throw rocks at the lake we realize that the rocks are behaving according to very clear principles that affect all rocks and lakes—but the rocks and our throwing arm don't tell us much about how the lake got here in the beginning (or where the rocks came from, for that matter). So we look for answers from the "Lake Creator" that had been left around the shore for us to pick up. Those instructions, we finally figure out, tell us more about the rocks and the lake than we could ever have understood by looking at the rocks or tossing them at the lake.

That's where the book of Genesis comes in. Here's a quick summary so far.

- The only omnipotent and omniscient Being in existence creates the "beginning" and the "heavens and the earth"—the space-matter-time universe in which we we now live.

- The initial universe came into being as an unorganized, totally dark, "formless and empty" watery matrix.

- The great Energizer then "moved" on the "waters," causing a rotational motion to be initiated. Light was then commanded by the Speaker-Namer, and the "evening and morning" time cycle was set. Dark was called "night" and light was called "day."

- An "expanse" was then inserted into the watery matrix, with half of the "waters" being held "above" the expanse, and the remainder kept below the expanse. However that was implemented, the result later proved to enable the earth's produce and its living organisms to live much longer and grow bigger than we are able to realize today.

- Once the basic structure of the universe was set, the Speaker-Namer commanded that the "waters under the expanse" gather together in one place, and the remainder to form dry land. The water was named "seas" and the land "earth."

- The great Creator was fully aware of His plan for the future, so He commanded: "Earth, sprout!" Accordingly, the basic dirt "produced" remarkable plant material that covered the dry land in grass, herbs, and trees. All of these widely varied types of "earth sprouts" were designed by the Creator-Speaker-Energizer to be "food" for the living creatures that would come two days later.

- In the design of the earth-sprouts, the Creator included instructions for reproduction and adaptation. That marvelous capacity, however, was limited. Grass could not become either herbs or trees, or vice versa. Everything that had those instructions "within" would only be able to do so "after its kind." Instead of a "tree" of common ancestry, a vast "lawn" of individual "kinds" was made out of the common "dirt" of earth.

As awesome and tantalizingly simple as this story is, the story holds together and fits all of the clear science that we can observe. The alternative story, however, is much more difficult to imagine. The precision of function and obvious design that we see around us in the universe is said to have "happened" by pure chance, rather than on purpose. Either the entire matter of the universe created itself by accident, or the eternal speck of total energy exploded a long time ago and set in motion random processes that produced order from the chaos.

The random, non-directed, chaotic explosion in the ancient eons produced purposeless and accidental forces by which the marvel of galaxies, planets, life, and civilizations came about. During the past two hundred years or so, mankind has learned a great deal more about the technical aspects of these random processes. We are now assured that even though all of this in the past was without any direction (or Director), mankind is now able to control and direct this evolution. God (or gods of any kind) is completely unnecessary.

Written records about such beginnings go back a few thousand years. Most of them insist that "the gods" fought and debated for eons before they could agree on how to get along. That religious thinking is laughingly discarded by many of the academics of our world because it implies direction and reason and the supernatural. That kind of thinking is absurd; except as it applies to "natural selection."

More, on both sides, could be said. But ultimately we are faced with believing one story's presuppositions over the other. Either an omnipotent and omniscient Creator-Speaker-Energizer did and does exist, or such a being is nothing more than the wishful thinking of ignorant men.

CHAPTER FOUR
THE BEGINNING OF THE SOLAR SYSTEM

One of the major conflicts surrounding the evolutionary ideas of natural forces causing the development of our solar system is that the Bible insists that the sun, moon and stars were all made on the fourth day of the creation week—after earth and all its plants were brought into existence. Surely, the argument insists, anyone with any sense knows that a planet could not exist prior to a sun, and it is foolish to accept such a naive story.

Those who express a confidence in the natural reading of the words of the Bible are often accused of being naïve. Such naïve readers would hold to the simplistic notion that God is omnipotent and omniscient, and that whatever He reveals is truthful. They believe that God is able to do what He said He did and that He is able to communicate what He meant to say about what He did! Unsophisticated? Perhaps, but any other view of the biblical text would place man's continually changing finite understanding in authority over whatever God said.

Of course, those who don't believe in any kind of God—especially a Creator God—do not have to deal with these issues at all.

Atheists can (and do) merely dump the message of Scripture into the wasteland of myth and legend. For those who attempt to escape the debate by claiming agnosticism, their non-logic is merely a shadowy haze of "don't know, don't care." Easy enough to discard the Bible's message if you are an atheist or an agnostic.

A Quick Review

The first day

The "beginning" (time), the "heavens" (space), and the "earth" (matter) were created instantaneously by omnipotent authority. The "formless and empty" universe came into existence as a dark watery matrix—dark because prior to the creation only the Triune God existed and "in him is no darkness at all" (1 John 1:5). "Light" (light energy) was inserted into the heavens and onto the earth by spoken command. The "north and the south" were created (Psalm 89:12), which surely involved the beginning of the rotation and magnetic fields of our planet.

Those processes made possible the "division" of the dark and the light (the night-day cycle), which founded the essential 24-hour "day" of our earthly existence. God named the light portion "day" and the dark portion "night," and noted that the "evening and the morning" were Day One. The entire structure of the initial cosmos was pronounced "good" by the all-powerful and all-knowing Creator Himself.

The second day

With the basic cosmology of time-space-matter in place, God makes an important structural change to the universe. He "divides" the waters into two distinct bodies by inserting an "expanse" into the rotating matrix. Some of the "waters" (perhaps one-half) were placed "above" the expanse, and the rest below. After dividing "the waters from the waters," God specifically named the expanse "heaven."

While it is not clear from the biblical data exactly what form the waters above the heaven were given, we have come to understand from the fossil record that the earth was ecologically and geographically very different in the past. Whatever God did on this second day, the effect was to make our planet more mild and habitable than we experience today. Evidence exists to verify that tropical plants and cold-blooded animals thrived all over the surface in ages past. Something structural enhanced that climate and permitted life to flourish well beyond the restrictions of environmental conditions today.

Later, the apostle Peter would tell us that the "world that then existed"—which was "standing out of water and in the water"—"perished, being flooded with water" (2 Peter 3:5-6). Obviously, from a biblical perspective, this was so significant that the Creator took an entire "evening and morning" to accomplish it.

The third day

The third "evening and morning" were very busy! Now that the earth had some sort of shield in the "heaven" that could protect and preserve the complex design of the Creator, the planet itself could be given organization and beauty.

First, the water and the "dirt" were separated into "seas" and "dry land." There is no indication in the information of Scripture of the shapes and sizes of the seas and continents. But the language used does indicate that some of the water was pooled into "fountains of the deep" that appear to have been the source for a "mist" that "watered the ground" instead of the hydrological cycle that we are familiar with today. Those fountains later erupted in a worldwide explosion to begin the horrible judgment of the Flood of Noah's day.

Once the planet's environmental structure was established, God "ordered" the earth to "sprout" and produce grass, herbs, and fruit trees. These marvelous and complex replicating systems were designed to have "seed" within themselves and to "fill" the earth "after their kind." Modern science is just beginning to understand something of the DNA and metabolic processes that continue to follow the Creator's design. But follow they do! Everything we *know* about the earth's flora verifies the basic statements of Genesis. Grass produces grass, and does not produce fruit trees. Fig trees don't produce grapes. Everything works just as God designed it to do—and told us that it would do!

Evolutionary science may imagine and spin sophisticated stories of how dirt became grass, but there has not ever been a scientific paper describing an observation of such a thing ever happening. Ever! As far as we know and observe, the first palm tree just leaped out of the dirt and produced fruit. The Bible tells us that God ordered it to happen just that way. We are faced with believing or not believing.

The fourth day

Now that the planet has been properly prepared, the earth is ready for its clocks. The space-matter-time universe has been created. The shield of "waters" has been put in place somewhere above the "heaven," and the earth itself has been developed with seas and lands and "food" for the living creatures that God has planned for the coming days. Although there is some "light" that streams into the creation and the dark is divided from the light in an "evening and morning" cycle, there is no way for the future inhabitants to understand the successive passage of time.

Thus, there must be a time-keeping system for "signs and seasons, and for days and years."

> Then God said, "Let there be lights in the firmament of the heavens to divide the day from the night; and let them be for signs and seasons, and for days and years; and let them be for lights in the firmament of the heavens to give light on the earth"; and it was so.
>
> Then God made two great lights: the greater light to rule the day, and the lesser light to rule the night. He made the stars also. God set them in the firmament of the heavens to give light on the earth, and to rule over the day and over the night, and to divide the light from the darkness. And God saw that it was good.

So the evening and the morning were the fourth day. (Genesis 1:14-19)

The lights of heaven

There is a play on words in the Hebrew text that is easy to miss with any translation. God describes the reason for His action: "Let them be for *lights* in the firmament of the heavens to give *light* on the earth." The word translated "lights" is *ma'owr*. The second term is *'owr*. Obviously, the terms are related, but they do have a significantly different application.

Ma'owr is used to represent the light holders, or light bearers. *'Owr* defines the essence of light itself—light energy, we might say; or perhaps, visible light. The "light holders" of Day Four are the "luminaries" (*ma'owr*) that carry or give off the "light" (*'owr*) that we see.

Perhaps a few references using *ma'owr* will help illustrate how the term is used.

- Exodus 13:21 – "a pillar of fire, to give them *light*"
- Leviticus 24:2 – "pure oil olive beaten for the *light*"
- Numbers 4:9 – "the candlestick of the *light*"
- Psalm 74:16 – "thou hast prepared the *light* and the sun"
- Ezekiel 32:8 – "all the bright *lights* of heaven"

In each of these references, "light" refers to the ability to hold or contain the "light" that enables us to see. The Lord specifically said of the sun and the moon that they were to "to give light on the earth." God "made" these light holders (as distinct from "created"). Apparently, God encapsulated the "light" of Day One into several different kinds of "luminaries" (see 1 Corinthians 15:41) and gave them the responsibility to "rule" the day and the night—and to set up a recognizable and reliable system for "signs and seasons, and for days and years."

For signs

When describing the purpose for these "luminaries" of the heavens, God insists that they are to be for "signs." The English word is sometimes used for a miraculous event or some observable sequence of events that foretells a coming event. In this case, the Hebrew word (*'owth*) is not normally used that way. Usually, *'owth* speaks of a "mark" or a "token" that identifies rather than foretells. Here are a few references that may help understand how God uses the term.

- Genesis 4:15 – "the LORD set a *mark* upon Cain"

- Genesis 9:12-13 – "I do set my bow in the cloud, and it shall be for a *token* of a covenant between me and the earth"

- Genesis 17:11 – "you shall be circumcised in the flesh of your foreskins, and it shall be a *sign* of the covenant between Me and you"

- Exodus 10:2 – that you may tell…the mighty things I have done in Egypt, and My *signs* which I have done among them, that you may know that I am the LORD"

- Exodus 12:13 – "the blood shall be to you for a *token* upon the houses"

- Exodus 31:17 – "observe the Sabbath…. It is a *sign* between Me and the children of Israel forever; for in six days the LORD made the heavens and the earth, and on the seventh day He rested and was refreshed."

- Isaiah 7:14 – "Therefore the Lord Himself will give you a *sign*: Behold, the virgin shall conceive and bear a Son, and shall call His name Immanuel."

Many more references could be cited, but these should suffice to illustrate that the purpose of the "lights" in the heavens were to *identify*, to *mark* the passage of time. They were, for instance, never intended to be some sort of astrological "sign" (miracle, foretelling). Nor was there ever any hint that these majestic "rulers" of the heavens were to be worshiped. The horrible rebellion of ancient Babel under Nimrod (Genesis 10 and 11) fell into that trap. The nation of Israel repeatedly "served other gods, and worshipped them, either the sun, or moon, or any of the host of heaven" (Deuteronomy 17:3).

No, these great "lights" in the heavens were to serve as "marks" of the passage of time.

For seasons

In addition to their role as "markers" for the passage of time, these "lights" were also to serve for "seasons." Again, the word choice is significant. The Hebrew term is *mow'ed* and specifies an "appointed" time. Here are a few references where *mow'ed* is used:

- Genesis 17:21 – "I establish with Isaac, which Sarah shall bear unto thee at this _set time_ in the next year"

- Exodus 23:15 – "thou shalt eat unleavened bread seven days, as I commanded thee, in the _time appointed_ of the month Abib"

- Jeremiah 8:7 – "the stork in the heaven knoweth her _appointed times_"

- Hosea 2:9 – "take away my corn in the time thereof, and my wine in _the season_ thereof"

As God placed these "luminaries" in the heavens, He designed them as "identifiers" of time passage, but He also orchestrated their design and function so that they would identify specifically "appointed" events during time. The most obvious is the time of the Messiah and the fulfillment of all the prophetic promises of history.

> But when the fullness of the time had come, God sent forth His Son, born of a woman, born under the law, to redeem those who were under the law, that we might receive the adoption as sons. (Galatians 4:4-5)

> Now when Jesus was born in Bethlehem of Judaea in the days of Herod the king, behold, there came wise men

from the east to Jerusalem, Saying, Where is he that is born King of the Jews? for we have seen his star in the east, and are come to worship him. (Matthew 2:1-2)

Although this discussion is not about the miraculous incarnation of our Lord Jesus—the Word made flesh—that event was "appointed" in the design of the Creator and was so significant that the "markers" of heaven provided a visible testimony of that appointment!

But the ordinary role of these lights in the heavens is far more common. So common, in fact, that we seldom give it much thought. "He appointed the moon for seasons; The sun knows its going down" (Psalm 104:19). Every passing day, every passing month, each turn of the seasons, we simply say, "That's the way it is," and other than an occasional grumble about changes in the weather, we ignore the marvelous stability of our planets' appointments.

Indeed, we know that earth is orbiting the sun and that her rotational cycle lets us experience the "evening and the morning." But we see and speak of the "sunset" and the "sunrise." We understand that the moon regulates the tides of our oceans, but we rarely give the Creator credit for "appointing" the moon to "rule" in that way. Science has begun to grasp the significance of the precise tilt of earth on her axis that provides the energy disbursement mechanism that enables the "seasons." But how often do we remember that the Creator promised, "While the earth remains, Seedtime and harvest, Cold and heat, Winter and summer, And day and night Shall not cease" (Genesis 8:22)?

For days and years

And therein lies the basic, everyday value of the "lights" in the heavens. Without them, especially without the sun to rule the day and the moon to rule the night, we would not be able to maintain any kind of schedule or orderly progress.

The Hebrew word translated "rule" is *memshalah*. This term speaks of a realm or a ruler. It is very different from the commands to "subdue" and "have dominion"—terms that were used to describe the stewardship authority given to mankind (Genesis 1:26, 28). The sun and the moon were to "have a realm of authority" defined by the Creator. The sun "presides" over the "day" and the moon "oversees" the "night." Neither one of them "subdues" or "has dominion" because man is delegated authority to "rule" the earth. Yet both of them clearly "preside" in their spheres of authority. No "normal" life would be possible without their continual and faithful function.

Suppose that God would have merely left the "light" of the first day beaming down from someplace outside the edge of the universe. We would have the "evening and morning" that existed from the beginning of Day One. But we would have no clear reference, no observable means of identifying the passage of time. Yes, there would be light and dark cycles, but no points to refer to, no phases of seasonal recognition, no "clock" to mark the greater spans of time.

- Genesis 5:5 – "all the days that Adam lived were nine hundred and thirty years: and he died"

- Psalm 90:9 – "The days of our lives are seventy years; And if by reason of strength they are eighty years"

- Galatians 4:10 – "You observe days and months and seasons and years"

The events of the fourth day were very important

He Made the Stars Also

The Bible reveals that there are enormous numbers of stars (Hebrews 11:12), and that they are all "named" by their Creator (Psalm 147:4) and are part of the "signs" (tokens) of the heavens (Genesis 1:14-16). Evidently they are to be both visible and identifiable. They are definitely not randomly scattered throughout space.

Modern astronomy has allowed us a glimpse into the awe-inspiring vistas of the universe. Everywhere we explore, more and more is revealed in space. The billions of stars in each of the billions of galaxies can only be expressed as "innumerable." When God gave His promise to Abraham about the uncounted nations that would come from him, God said that the stars of the heavens and the sand of the seashore were comparable illustrations (Genesis 22:17).

Some studies have been conducted to calculate the number of grains of sand potentially in the earth (average size of sand grains multiplied by the average number of grains in a cubic meter of sand times the cubic thickness of the earth's crust), and the numbers are fairly close to the calculated numbers of the stars! God wasn't just using hyperbole, He was speaking as the One who created both the sand and the stars.

And each of the multiplied billions and billions of named stars has order, purpose, and identifying roles to play. When God spoke to Job, He insisted that Job ought to be able to observe the specified order in Pleiades and Orion, and that the seasonal changes in the "Mazzaroth" (the twelve divisions) were common knowledge, as well as the easily recognized "ordinances of heaven" (Job 38:31-33).

Not one of these uncountable stellar "lights" was developed over eons of time. "By the word of the LORD the heavens were made, and all the host of them by the breath of His mouth....For He spoke, and it was done; He commanded, and it stood fast" (Psalm 33:6, 9).

The Solar System Speaks

> The heavens declare the glory of God; and the firmament shows His handiwork. Day unto day utters speech, and night unto night reveals knowledge. There is no speech nor language where their voice is not heard. Their line has gone out through all the earth, and their words to the end of the world. In them He has set a tabernacle for the sun, which is like a bridegroom coming out of his chamber, and rejoices like a strong man to run its race. Its rising is from one end of heaven, and its circuit to the other end; and there is nothing hidden from its heat. (Psalm 19:1-6)

Whatever is designed into the vast heavens, there is certainly the "speech" and "knowledge" of the Creator. Written like a huge signature across the stellar universe is a "language" that speaks clearly to every human being over all time and in all cultures. The apostle Paul, perhaps the best educated intellectual of the New Testament writers, stunned the sophisticated scholars and world leaders of his day by noting:

> Since the creation of the world His invisible attributes are clearly seen, being understood by the things that are made, even His eternal power and Godhead, so that they are without excuse. (Romans 1:20)

Like the psalmist a millennium before, both writers insisted that there was a continual streaming communication from the Creator that made aspects of His attributes so clear that anyone who questioned the reality of an omnipotent and omniscient Creator was "without excuse."

Two competing messages

There are essentially only two "stories" about how the universe came to be. Both are not provable by testing and observation. Both are presuppositional belief systems, based on personal preference. Once embraced however, they shape the thinking processes so strongly that all evidence is "interpreted" to suit the previously embraced presupposition.

The "naturalist" must assume that either no God exists or that if such a being does exist he has nothing to do with what exists. Such a person must look at the universe and devise a "story" of how such "apparent" order and complexity came about through randomness and chaos. Some of those stores are actually quite sophisticated and often sound plausible, given enough time for random forces to form something of substance and coordinated power, all by chance.

But the creationist will look at the same universe and marvel at the evidence for the "eternal power" so obviously displayed among the galaxies.

The First Cause

One of the most obvious laws of all science is called "the Law of Cause and Effect." All human experience understands that whenever anything happens (an event), something previous to that event was the "cause" of that event. Nothing just "happens" by itself. All science knows that matter cannot be created or destroyed. So, here's the problem. If matter (mass-energy) is incapable of creating itself, and all matter was caused by something, then there must be an initial "Cause" that can account for the entire mass-energy of the universe—and that Cause must be omnipotent.

That same problem exists for the absolutely staggering amount of complexity and order in the universe. No matter whether we look "up" into the universe at the galaxies or "down" into the microscopic volumes of information in the DNA, something must have enough information to "cause" such immeasurable information—an omniscient Cause.

Our special solar system

Brian Thomas, one of the science writers of the Institute for Creation Research, released a short summary of how special our solar system is compared to the rest of the planets that we know about outside our own.

> New research is shedding surprising light on the uniqueness of our solar system. Over 250 planet-like objects (mostly gas giants) have been observed in distant space, and researchers are curious about how they formed and how they compare with earth and its neighboring planets.
>
> For decades, astronomers have popularized the "nebular hypothesis," which asserts that planets were formed by the gravitational attraction of dust particles to space rocks. The dust presumably existed in a disk surrounding newly-formed stars. Despite numerous major problems

with this theory, it is still prominently featured in science textbooks.

If the 8 official solar planets (with their over 130 satellites) and the 250 extrasolar planet-like objects were all formed by dust accretion, it would be logical to assume that they should exhibit similar characteristics. But new research from Northwestern University is finding that extrasolar planets don't look like our local planets at all.

Computer modeling studies based on the nebular hypothesis show that the formation of planets like those in our solar system would require a unique series of special parameters to keep them from flying off into space, crashing into the sun, entering extremely elliptical (non-circular) orbits, orbiting so near the sun that their solar year would take only days, or ending up too small to be much more than an asteroid or too large, thus becoming a star.

Why didn't the planets of our solar system fly off into space? In the study that appears in the August 8, 2008, issue of the journal *Science*, one Northwestern researcher suggests it could be due to "dynamical friction from the remnant outer planetesimal disk...serving to prevent their ejection and ultimately recircularize their orbits." In other words, leftover space junk supposedly nudged not just one, but all 9 of our traditional planets into their circular orbits.

Could random "friction" have resulted in the precise alignment of our planets? If so, why hasn't this occurred anywhere else in the known universe? As the senior author of the *Science* paper states, "The shapes of the exoplanets' orbits are elongated, not nice and circular. Planets are not where we expect them to be. Many giant planets similar to Jupiter, known as 'hot Jupiters,' are so close to the star they have orbits of mere days. Clearly we needed to start fresh in explaining planetary formation and this greater variety of planets we now see."

According to the Northwestern study, our solar system appears to be pretty "special." It could even be described as well-designed. The book of Genesis recounts the creation of the sun, moon, and stars. If its narrative account is true, then of course we would expect the handiwork of this Creator to be pretty special.[1]

Clear Words – Simple Language

Most of our Bible-believing forefathers were quite naïve, of course. They had the simplistic notion that God was omnipotent and truthful. In their unsophisticated view of things, they believed that the Bible was God's Word and that He was able to do what He said He did, and that He said what He meant to say about what He did! They believed what He wrote when He wrote the Ten Commandments on "two tablets of stone written with the finger of God, and on them were all the words which the LORD had spoken to you on the mountain from the midst of the fire in the day of the assembly" (Deuteronomy 9:10).

Among the words that God wrote with His own finger were these: "Six days you shall labor and do all your work, but the seventh day is the Sabbath of the LORD your God…. For in six days the LORD made the heavens and the earth, the sea, and all that is in them, and rested the seventh day" (Exodus 20:9-11). Everything that was in the heavens was made in that primeval six-day period, or, more specifically, on the fourth day of that period when God had said that He "made two great lights, the greater light to rule the day, and the lesser light to rule the night: He made [note, not "is making"] the stars also."

That seems easy enough to understand. God was surely able to do that, and that's what He says He did! "By the word of the LORD the heavens were made, And all the host of them by the breath of His mouth…. For He spoke, and it was done; He commanded, and it

---

1   Brian Thomas, Astronomers Speak: Our Solar System Is "Special," *ICR News,* posted on icr.org August 14, 2008.

stood fast" (Psalm 33:6-9). "Thus the heavens and the earth, and all the host of them, were finished. And on the seventh day God ended His work which He had done" (Genesis 2:1-2). Why are "finished" and "ended" so hard to understand?

Other ideas

One can understand why atheistic and pantheistic astronomers and cosmologists would reject this truth—the very premise of their profession requires them to try to understand the cosmos without invoking a Creator God. But Christian astronomers who say they believe in God and the Bible should find no problem with it.

Now, however, we have the phenomenon of Christian "apologists"—including at least one prominent communicator with a Ph.D. in astronomy—telling Christians they must abandon the biblical literalism of their forefathers. This otherwise intelligent Christian attempts to explain the cosmos through some 15 billion years of stellar evolution, starting with the hypothetical Big Bang, followed by the evolution of the elements, then the stars, galaxies, and planets. We ourselves are said to be the eventual product of these eons of stellar evolution, the elements of our very bodies being essentially "stardust" formed in ancient stellar processes.

Furthermore, they say, we can still see stellar evolution taking place in the heavens. We can see stars, galaxies, and planets in various stages of this cosmic evolutionary process.

Actually, no, we cannot! The heavens and the earth were "finished." All of God's heavenly "works were finished from the foundation of the world" (Hebrews 4:3). As long as people have been looking at the stars, they have never seen a single star evolve. We do occasionally see stars disintegrate, but that's not evolution. The tragedy is that so many leaders of Christian colleges, publications, churches, and para-church organizations are blindly following these latter-day apologists for modern scientism.

Inflation and quantum fluctuation

Perhaps the greatest anomaly in this situation is the incredibly weak scientific case for the whole scenario of cosmic evolution. There can be no "experiments" or "observations" of stars evolving, in the very nature of the case, so any theory cannot really be scientific, though it may be naturalistic—i.e., all based on mathematical manipulations, computer simulations, and atheistic or pantheistic philosophies.

Secular scientists are putting too much faith in these speculations. Some astronomers communicating with each other about these ideas among the various journals suggest that cosmologists should not take each other too seriously when they venture concepts about the universe in the first second after the Big Bang. Even the existence of the Big Bang itself depends on the extrapolation of physical principles and theories right back to the very beginning. These "religious concepts" in many of the popular cosmologies are not based on the scientific method.

Inflation theory

In spite of the great faith placed by certain Christian leaders in the Big Bang, there are many secular astronomers who reject it. Among the more obvious difficulties are its contradiction of the two universal laws of thermodynamics, but there are many others.

The "inflation theory" was enthusiastically promoted for a while in the 1980s as a means of resolving at least some of these problems. This was the notion that an incredibly small mini-universe "inflated" to the size of a grapefruit in an incredibly short time before it exploded into the Big Bang, which then proceeded to evolve into everything else. But inflation itself has encountered numerous problems, with many modifications having to be appended to the theory. Even so, there is no proof that inflation is correct and, to add to the uncertainty, distinct versions of the theory have proliferated as physicists grapple with the problem of finding an inflation that could have produced the universe but is also compatible with known laws of physics.

Nobody knows whether inflation actually happened. The idea is just that! An idea.

Since simple inflation turned out to be inadequate to generate the Big Bang and the cosmos, various cosmo-physicists have tried to improve on inflation. The theory now comes in varieties called old, new, chaotic, hybrid, and open inflation, with numerous subdivisions like supersymmetric, supernatural, and hyperextended inflation, each a vision of just how the inflation might have touched off the birth of the universe we see today.

What a delightful set of science rules. If your idea doesn't work, or can't be tested, or can't even be proven mathematically—then just come up with an exception that seems to take care of the problem intellectually. Then if that still doesn't work, invent something else!

Of course, there is the problem of what started the inflation in the first place.

Quantum fluctuation

This question has led to an even more fantastic speculation. There has somehow been a "quantum fluctuation" from nothing into something, by virtue of the uncertainty principle. One of the consequences of the uncertainty principle is that a region of seemingly empty space is not really empty, but is a seething froth in which every sort of fundamental particle pops out of empty space for a brief instant before annihilating with its antiparticle and disappearing—these are the so-called quantum fluctuations.

Atheistic astronomers used to replace Genesis 1:1 with their version of origins as: "In the beginning, hydrogen." But that didn't really explain the hydrogen. Now, the new version has it as follows: "In the beginning, quantum fluctuations." By no means, however, have we yet seen the end of these cosmic metaphysical speculations. Some scientists are really excited by the thought that this "quantum" approach to thinking might liberate them to great ideas beyond the foundational theories of Einstein's General Relativity.

Who knows? Perhaps they will someday even hit on the simplest of all—"In the beginning God created the heaven and the earth" (Genesis 1:1).

What Is Man?

Every thinking human being (usually as a child) has looked up into the night sky and echoed the silent cry of King David so long ago: "When I consider Your heavens, the work of Your fingers, the moon and the stars, which You have ordained, what is man that You are mindful of him, and the son of man that You visit him?" (Psalm 8:3-4).

The human answer to that question would dump all of us into an irrelevant fog of insignificance. The great omnipotent and omniscient Creator is so far beyond our pitiful and finite state that we should expect nothing but disdain or destruction from Him. Fortunately, one of the reasons that the Creator set forth to create was to make a being like Him that would be given the responsibility to manage the creation.

> Then God said, "Let Us make man in Our image, according to Our likeness; let them have dominion over the fish of the sea, over the birds of the air, and over the cattle, over all the earth and over every creeping thing that creeps on the earth." (Genesis 1:26)

That steward did rebel, and the unifying theme of the Bible demonstrates the Creator's unceasing love toward mankind, so that man can understand that "God demonstrates His own love toward us, in that while we were still sinners, Christ died for us" (Romans 5:8).

The great evidence of the creation is one of the clearest demonstrations of the sufficiency of the power of God to reclaim and reconcile us to Himself. When we look at the wonder of the creation, we should have all the more confidence that God is able to make a "new man which was created according to God, in true righteousness and holiness" (Ephesians 4:24).

Henry M. Morris III

Everything about the fourth day is designed to "identify" the "appointments" of God. Perhaps the greatest message is recognized in a portion of Psalm 136:6-8.

> To Him who made great lights, For His mercy endures forever—
>
> The sun to rule by day, For His mercy endures forever;
>
> The moon and stars to rule by night, For His mercy endures forever.

CHAPTER FIVE
THE BEGINNING OF LIFE

The fifth day of the creation week introduces us to life. Day Three brought into existence the "food" of earth—the reproducing plants that were to be the source of nourishment for all living things. It should be noted again that these "sprouts" of the earth were not simple in any sense of the word, and they were designed by the Creator to have enormous flexibility among their "kind" to "fill" the earth. The products of the "dirt" of earth vary in size, function, relationships, adaptability, and use.

Exceedingly complex in molecular structure, they are widely flexible within their DNA potential. They are limited to adaptability "after their kind." They are both beautiful and "good for food."

But they are not alive!

Yes, we are well aware that modern science treats the study of botany as though flora are alive. However the biblical text does not. Although the discussion of these issues may seem like a minor debate—something for a group of theological and scientific scholars to dispute in their private club room—in fact, this is of major biblical importance.

There are number of alternative "creation" theories—all espoused *only* by Christian groups that insist that the creation week described in the biblical text must be interpreted in some way to accommodate naturalistic science. The common denominator among all of those various "isms" is that the "days" of Genesis 1 were not 24-hour periods, but were varying ages of developmental evolutionary processes guided or helped by God in some way. All these accommodations to evolutionary naturalism insist that the processes took billions of years.

Integral to all of these theories is that death is a "normal" and "necessary" part of the process—just as atheistic naturalism insists. Death is the "good" process of all living things that eliminates the less fit or the developing and not yet fully functional forms of life, so that God can achieve His intended "design" at the end of the ages-long process.

Part and parcel to embracing the ages-long evolutionary processes of modern science, these hybrid theories all insist that plants are "alive" and that, therefore, when other animals and eventually man eat the plants, they are "killing" the plants—hence "death" is an acceptable part of God's design.

Dominant Secular Philosophies

Perhaps it would be helpful to quickly review the dominant secular philosophies that have influenced human thinking since the rise of the Enlightenment of the 18th century.

Atheism

Many will recognize the names of Nietzsche, Marx, Huxley, and Sartre—atheistic philosophers who changed the world with their ideas about living a godless life. Apart from required reading in college, most Christians couldn't care less about the influence of these lauded thinkers of the past. And yet the effects of their ideas are seen throughout societies everywhere.

Marx and Engels, for example, established the principles of communism, an atheistic philosophy and political system that brought misery upon multiple millions around the world during the 20th century. They still dominate the peoples of China, Cuba, North Korea, and other despotic regimes today. America itself has been infiltrated by atheism, and universities have become the breeding ground for these ideas.

The following excerpt from a speech delivered at Memphis State University by the renowned Madalyn Murray O'Hair, founder of American Atheists, clearly expresses the essence of modern atheism:

> This is your life: What you see is what you get. If you are going to make your life better for yourself—the task is yours. If you want to make the world better for all its inhabitants—all animals, all life forms, all vegetation—you need to work on it. There needs to be a scientific analysis of what we have, what we want, and how to get from one point to another. No god ever gave any man anything, nor answered any prayer, nor ever will.
>
> American Atheists, whom I represent, asks you simply to understand that the proper study of man is mankind. We can attain any number of utopian plateaus as we reach for a commonsense goal which attracted many to our nation: the greatest good for the greatest number. We can reach this goal through education, the scientific method of evaluation, planning, and work. Religion has caused more misery to all of humankind in every age of history than any other single idea. You need to be free of irrational ideas. You need to repudiate those who would attempt to return you to medievalism. You need to look forward, not backward; you need to strive for intellectual freedom, not mental bondage; you need to seek joy, not sorrow; love, not fear; and you can do that only when you realize who and what your oppressor was—and is.

Practical, modern atheism depends upon man to reach utopia. Religion—theism—is an enemy of mankind's successful development. This godless living is naturalism. Atheism is the belief system that claims to know that there never was, is not now, or never will be a god of any kind, let alone one Supreme Being, found in or beyond the known world. Nature, with man as its supreme being, is the extent of what exists.

Eliminating God eliminates the Creator, which eliminates any semblance of absolute authority over the world. Thus mankind is free to choose his own authority—himself. As his own supreme authority, man now has the ability to decide what is true and what is not true. This resultant "truth" is now accepted as the best of what can be known. And this has become the foundation—the worldview—of modern, naturalistic science.

No God, no Creator, no authority, no accountability, no absolutes.

Humanism

Humanism is a "system of thought that rejects religious beliefs and centers on humans and their values, capacities, and worth."

This man-centered "religion" is merely a philosophical restatement of naturalism, focused on the role that man has reached as the highest pinnacle of evolutionary processes. It is also a restatement of Lucifer's twisted lie in the Garden of Eden that "ye shall be as gods, knowing good and evil" (Genesis 3:5). Although this so-called egalitarian philosophy purports to be a "vibrant, satisfying faith," it becomes a "struggle for existence" that favors the bold, the arrogant, and the egotistical. History is littered with despots, tyrants, and bigots who oiled their way into power with "humanistic" slogans.

But because humanism is not universally accepted—many still believe in some sort of Supreme Being—the modern humanist movement has as its prime objective to abolish organized religion, to abolish throughout society the idea that there is anything or anyone higher than mankind (i.e., God), and to magnify man as a self-appointed deity.

Consider these statements from the Humanist Manifesto III:

- Humanism is a progressive philosophy of life that, without supernaturalism, affirms our ability and responsibility to lead ethical lives of personal fulfillment that aspire to the greater good of humanity.

- Knowledge of the world is derived by observation, experimentation, and rational analysis.

- Humans are an integral part of nature, the result of unguided evolutionary change.

- Ethical values are derived from human need and interest as tested by experience.

- Life's fulfillment emerges from individual participation in the service of humane ideals.

- Humans are social by nature and find meaning in relationships.

- Working to benefit society maximizes individual happiness.

- The responsibility for our lives and the kind of world in which we live is ours and ours alone.

Humanism is atheistic. Man, therefore, becomes the supreme being in the universe.

Materialism

Materialism is the belief that "nothing exists except matter—things that can be measured or known through the senses. Materialists deny the existence of spirit, and they look for physical explanations for all phenomena. Thus, for example, they trace mental states to the brain or nervous system, rather than to the spirit or the soul. Marxism, because it sees human culture as the product of economic forces, is a materialist system of beliefs."

Karl Marx and Friedrich Engles wrote in their book *The German Ideology*:

The first premise of all human history is, of course, the existence of living human individuals. Thus the first fact to be established is the physical organization of these individuals and their consequent relation to the rest of nature.

Men can be distinguished from animals by consciousness, by religion or anything else you like. They themselves begin to distinguish themselves from animals as soon as they begin to produce their means of subsistence, a step which is conditioned by their physical organization. By producing their means of subsistence men are indirectly producing their actual material life.

The way in which men produce their means of subsistence depends first of all on the nature of the actual means of subsistence they find in existence and have to reproduce. This mode of production must not be considered simply as being the production of the physical existence of the individuals. Rather it is a definite form of activity of these individuals, a definite form of expressing their life, a definite mode of life on their part. As individuals express their life, so they are. What they are, therefore, coincides with their production, both with what they produce and with how they produce. The nature of individuals thus depends on the material conditions determining their production.[1]

This rather confusing philosophical maze attempts to explain that man distinguishes himself from other forms of nature only as he produces his own "subsistence." In other words, man evolves himself into whatever he wants to make of himself.

In short, materialism sees man as simply one part of nature, not necessarily as a special part of nature. The individual man becomes irrelevant in the big picture. Even though nature includes man, it is supreme over the individual since nature is "all there is."

---

1   Karl Marx, 1938, Idealism and Materialism, in *The German Ideology*, London: Lawrence and Wishart.

The mystical form of materialism is pantheism. The various "New Age" movements, including the Eastern religions, see "god" in everything—hence, god is everything. Some movements personify the cosmos (like the "all soul" of Buddhism), but most pantheistic philosophies merely tie the "oneness" of the universe to a "force" (e.g., *Star Wars*) that permeates everything. Such materialistic pantheism is the rationale behind fringe environmental movements like Greenpeace and PETA (People for the Ethical Treatment of Animals).

More mystical forms like Wicca (neopagan witchcraft) and Gaea (worship of Mother Earth) and Vegans (exclusion of any animal product for food or clothing) base their practices on equating matter—particularly the living—as "divine" in one form or another.

This is "spiritual" atheism. If everything is god, then nothing is God.

What Is Life?

Obviously, every form of evolutionary naturalism views "life" as anything that is capable of cellular reproduction. The so-called "common ancestor" is supposed to be the first "life" and is said to be something like algae. All evolutionary schemes postulate some form of a "tree" of life that originates with this first life form, and then develops over ages through random natural processes to produce what is observed and recorded today.

The biblical text certainly presents a different view life.

Life is created

Three key Hebrew verbs were discussed in part during Chapter 2. One, *'asah*, was the common term for making or doing something. *'Asah* is always used in a context where it is clear that the "doer" is using material already available and performing some innovative or augmentative technique on that material to produce something more specific for a designed purpose. We could easily understand that an engineer "makes" a bridge or a highway or a piece of construction equipment. His training and skill enables him to take existing materials and connect them such a way that a "new" product is made. Such a person is *'asah*-ing.

Yatsar is another of those key Hebrew verbs. Although this verb is a "making" verb, it is a much more personal verb than *'asah*. *Yatsar* implies a hands-on involvement, and connotes the personal attention of the "doer." "We might use this verb to speak of what an artist does when he paints a picture or sculpts a figure. This is the verb that the Bible text uses to describe what the Creator did when He made Adam. "And the LORD God *formed* man of the dust of the ground, and breathed into his nostrils the breath of life; and man became a living being" (Genesis 2:7). In another place we are told: "He who planted the ear, shall He not hear? He who *formed* the eye, shall He not see?" (Psalm 94:9).

But men can *yatsar* as well.

> Who would *form* a god or mold an image that profits him nothing? The blacksmith with the tongs works one in the coals, *Fashions* it with hammers, And works it with the strength of his arms. Even so, he is hungry, and his strength fails; He drinks no water and is faint. (Isaiah 44:10, 12)

While there is certainly a great gulf between the making and forming of men and the work of the Creator, the activity is not unique to God.

Bārā', however, is the one verb clearly intended to describe God's unique power to bring something into existence where nothing existed before. A few obvious examples should suffice.

> Genesis 1:1 – In the beginning God *created* the heavens and the earth.

> Genesis 1:27 – So God *created* man in His own image; in the image of God He *created* him; male and female He *created* them.

> Exodus 34:10 – And He said: "Behold, I make a cove-

nant. Before all your people I will do marvels such as have not been _done_ in all the earth, nor in any nation; and all the people among whom you are shall see the work of the LORD. For it is an awesome thing that I will do with you."

Psalm 51:10 – _Create_ in me a clean heart, O God, And renew a steadfast spirit within me.

Psalm 89:12 – The north and the south, You have _created_ them; Tabor and Hermon rejoice in Your name.

Isaiah 40:26 – Lift up your eyes on high, And see who has _created_ these things, Who brings out their host by number; He calls them all by name, By the greatness of His might And the strength of His power; Not one is missing.

Isaiah 40:28 – Have you not known? Have you not heard? The everlasting God, the LORD, The _Creator_ of the ends of the earth, Neither faints nor is weary. His understanding is unsearchable.

Isaiah 42:5 – Thus says God the LORD, Who _created_ the heavens and stretched them out, Who spread forth the earth and that which comes from it, Who gives breath to the people on it, And spirit to those who walk on it.

Jeremiah 31:22 – How long will you gad about, O you backsliding daughter? For the LORD has _created_ a new thing in the earth—A woman shall encompass a man.

Amos 4:13 – For behold, He who forms mountains, And _creates_ the wind, Who declares to man what his thought is, And makes the morning darkness, Who treads the high places of the earth—The LORD God of hosts is His name.

The term appears 54 times in the Hebrew text of the Old Testament. God is the only subject of the verb in the overwhelming majority of those appearances. Joshua uses the word twice to describe the work of a Tribe of Israel clearing an area for them to settle in during the period of conquest (Joshua 17:15, 18). God tells Ezekiel to "make" a sign that will point Babylon on the right road so they can execute God's judgment on Israel (Ezekiel 21:19). And in one awful passage of judgment, God tells Ezekiel what will happen to those who have despised God's Word—that the people whom they have led into sin will "execute" them (Ezekiel 23:47). Other than these four figurative uses of the word, it is absolutely clear from the biblical text that God is the Creator who "creates" something from nothing using power and processes that we know nothing about.

> Hebrews 11:3 – By faith we understand that the worlds were framed by the word of God, so that the things which are seen were not made of things which are visible.

> Romans 4:17 – ...God, who gives life to the dead and calls those things which do not exist as though they did.

The New Testament stresses the creative power of God applied to the twice-born process that "creates" an eternal life where nothing existed but something that was "dead in trespasses and sins" (Ephesians 2:1). All of self-conscious life will one day acknowledge that such action is unique to the "Alpha and Omega" of eternity. All will worship and confess that God alone is able to "create"—Man is the created, not the Creator.

> Revelation 4:11 – You are worthy, O Lord, to receive glory and honor and power; For You created all things, And by Your will they exist and were created.

In simple language, only God can "create" life.

Life is unique

Obviously, animal and human life is different from the plants and vegetation of earth. But we have so co-mingled the terms that we often overlook the fact that the Bible text uses a unique word for "life" that is never applied to plants and vegetation.

The first use of such a term is in Genesis 1:20-30 where God describes His creative action on Day Five. The word choice of the Holy Spirit is *chay* (and its derivatives) and occasionally the word *chayah*.

Together those words are used 763 times in the Old Testament—never applying that quality to plants or vegetation.

> Then God said, "Let the waters abound with an abundance of *living creatures*, and let birds fly above the earth across the face of the firmament of the heavens." So God created great sea creatures and every *living thing* that moves, with which the waters abounded, according to their kind, and every winged bird according to its kind. And God saw that it was good....Then God said, "Let the earth bring forth the *living* creature according to its kind: cattle and creeping thing and *beast* of the earth, each according to its kind"; and it was so. And God made the *beast* of the earth according to its kind, cattle according to its kind, and everything that creeps on the earth according to its kind. And God saw that it was good....Then God blessed them, and God said to them, "Be fruitful and multiply; fill the earth and subdue it; have dominion over the fish of the sea, over the birds of the air, and over every *living thing* that moves on the earth....Also, to every *beast* of the earth, to every bird of the air, and to everything that creeps on the earth, in which there is *life* I have given every green herb for food"; and it was so. (Genesis 1:20-30)

Please note that last phrase. The "beasts" and the "birds" and the "living creatures" and the various "creeping things" are to find "food" from the "green herb."" In no place in the Scriptures are plants ascribed the "life" that "living" creatures possess. Plants are food. They do not possess the life of animals and man. They are, indeed, marvelous and beautiful and complex and able to reproduce "after their kind," but they are designed by the Creator to be a source of energy to maintain life—they are *not* alive.

Life has independent movement

This may seem like either an obvious point or an irrelevant one.

However, one of the descriptive terms that the Creator applied to living creatures was "movement."

> Genesis 1:21 – So God created great sea creatures and every living thing that _moves_ with which the waters abounded, according to their kind, and every winged bird according to its kind. And God saw that it was good.

> Genesis 1:26 – Then God said, "Let Us make man in Our image, according to Our likeness; let them have dominion over the fish of the sea, over the birds of the air, and over the cattle, over all the earth and over every creeping thing that _creeps_ on the earth."

> Genesis 1:28 – Then God blessed them, and God said to them, "Be fruitful and multiply; fill the earth and subdue it; have dominion over the fish of the sea, over the birds of the air, and over every living thing that _moves_ on the earth."

> Genesis 1:30 – Also, to every beast of the earth, to every bird of the air, and to everything that _creeps_ on the earth, in which there is life, I have given every green herb for food; and it was so.

The Hebrew word is _ramas_, used 17 times in the Old Testament—never of plants or vegetation of any kind. It is used to describe birds gliding through the atmosphere. It is used of insects "sneaking" around on the floor of the earth. It is used of large beasts "stalking" and moving freely through the wild lands of the earth. It is never used of trees, or plants, or grass, or vegetation of any kind.

Living things move. Not just swaying to the wind movement; not just spores drifting along or pollen hitching a ride on bees, but independent, conscious, willful movement. Almost all plants are "rooted" to the earth—they are "sprouts" of earth. Living things eat plants! Plants do not travel from one location to another—except on the backs of animals or in trucks driven by men! They are "rooted!" They do not have the power of _ramas_.

Science has had an interesting time trying to sort out some of the smallest of "moving things." Most of us have looked down a microscope tube at the "wigglies" in a drop of pond water. They are amazing critters! Some of them ooze (like the amoeba), others bounce around like the paramecium. And if we are able to watch long enough, we can see them split into two—reproduce right in front of our very eyes! Fascinating!

But there are real questions about the myriads in the microscopic domain. Most scientists would appear to agree that bacteria are alive (that is, they move and reproduce rather normally). Viruses, on the other hand, don't seem to behave at all like bacteria. In many ways viruses are more dangerous and we have a much more difficult time controlling or overcoming their harmful effects on living bodies. Lots of work still needs to be done to make sense of what we are beginning to understand of "the pestilence that walks in darkness" (Psalm 91:6).

But what we do know—what we have observed and tested repeatedly—is that living things have the ability to move independently and plants do not.

Life has blood

"The life of the flesh is in the blood," so announces Leviticus 17:11. There is so much in the Scriptures about the significance of blood as the evidence of life, it seems somewhat superfluous to speak of it. The bulk of the sacrificial system under Mosaic Law was centered in blood sacrifice. Again and again the dictates required the "shedding of blood" to kill (execute) the innocent animal in a temporary substitutionary atonement (covering) of the sins committed.

The whole Christian gospel is founded on the necessity of the shedding of the Messiah's blood during the crucifixion as evidence that His life was given on behalf of the "sins of the whole world" (1 John 2:2). The death of Jesus Christ was made necessary. "For it is not possible that the blood of bulls and goats could take away sins" (Hebrews 10:4). Surely the reader is aware of these broad and oft-repeated principles.

When God was instructing Noah about his responsibilities after the global Flood of cosmos-destroying judgment, God insisted that "you shall not eat flesh with its life, that is, its blood" (Genesis 9:4). The sacred "life" that was contained in the blood was so important that God even insisted that "surely for your lifeblood I will demand a reckoning; from the hand of every beast I will require it, and from the hand of man. From the hand of every man's brother I will require the life of man" (Genesis 9:5).

The dietary laws of the nation of Israel specifically restricted any consumption of blood in their meals. The blood was the life source of all living things, and was, therefore, to be held sacred.

> Leviticus 17:14 – for it is the life of all flesh. Its blood sustains its life. Therefore I said to the children of Israel, "You shall not eat the blood of any flesh, for the life of all flesh is its blood. Whoever eats it shall be cut off."

> Deuteronomy 12:23 – Only be sure that you do not eat the blood, for the blood is the life; you may not eat the life with the meat.

Those restrictions were a far cry from the blood drinks and blood puddings of the pagan societies of their day—not to mention the practice of bloodletting that abounded from ancient pagan Egypt until the "enlightenment" of naturalism and medical practice of our own "Christian" country. A foolish and rebellious rejection of the clear teachings of Scripture, one that sickened and killed millions over many centuries.

The concept was pretty simple. If a "moving creature" had blood, it was alive. If it had blood, it had life. Not very difficult to understand, but often either ignored or disputed.

Life has nephesh

This Hebrew word is used 753 times in the Old Testament and is translated by the English word "soul" 475 times. Another 117 times the translators chose "life" as the best way to express the term, but there is no doubt that the basic idea of the term is that *nephesh* speaks of the non-corporeal part of life—perhaps best equated with the self-conscious awareness that "I" exist. Frequently *nephesh* seems to be used to express the emotive side of living things as opposed to the thinking side of life.

> Psalm 35:9 – And my *soul* shall be joyful in the LORD; It shall rejoice in His salvation.

> Proverbs 14:10 – The heart knows its *own* bitterness, And a stranger does not share its joy.

> Isaiah 61:10 – I will greatly rejoice in the LORD, My *soul* shall be joyful in my God; For He has clothed me with the garments of salvation, He has covered me with the robe of righteousness, As a bridegroom decks himself with ornaments, And as a bride adorns herself with her jewels.

Nephesh is often used in the same context as the "heart" of man—that mysterious inner part of us that responds and reacts to events as well as seems to be the place where we make (or at least treasure) long-term commitments.

> Deuteronomy 4:9 – Only take heed to yourself, and diligently keep *yourself* (*nephesh*), lest you forget the things your eyes have seen, and lest they depart from your heart all the days of your life.

> Deuteronomy 6:5 – You shall love the LORD your God with all your heart, with all your *soul*, and with all your strength.

> 1 Chronicles 22:19 – Now set your heart and your *soul* to seek the LORD your God.

> Proverbs 23:7 – For as he thinks in his *heart* (*nephesh*), so is he. "Eat and drink!" he says to you, But his heart is not with you.

> Hosea 4:8 – They eat up the sin of My people; They set their *heart* (*nephesh*), on their iniquity.

Whether *nephesh* is translated by soul or life or person or mind or heart or creature or yourselves or desire or appetite, *nephesh* is never used of plants. Ever.

Life has ruwach

The other non-corporal term used by the Holy Spirit to describe and define life is the Hebrew word *ruwach*. Of the 389 times the word or its derivatives appear in the text of the Old Testament, it is translated "spirit" 232 times, "wind" 92 times, and "breath" 27 times. The clearest connection between *ruwach* and "life" is the phrase "breath of life."

> Genesis 6:17 – And behold I Myself am bringing flood-waters on the earth to destroy from under heaven all flesh in which is the *breath* (*ruwach*) of life; everything that is on the earth shall die.

> Genesis 7:15 – And they went into the ark to Noah, two by two, of all flesh in which is the *breath* (*ruwach*) of life.

> Genesis 7:22 – All in whose nostrils was the *breath* (*ruwach*) of the spirit of life all that was on the dry land, died.

These sweeping statements, made by God Himself and by Noah who witnessed the events, are clearly inclusive of every kind of living creature that lived on the dry land and breathed air. The only creatures that would not have been included would have been plants, marine animals, and some insects that neither breathe air nor have blood (as we know it).

Several passages suggest that the "spirit" of man and of animals is more than merely the ability to breathe.

> Psalm 32:2 – Blessed is the man to whom the LORD does not impute iniquity, And in whose *spirit* (*ruwach*) there is no deceit.

> Proverbs 16:2 – All the ways of a man are pure in his own eyes, But the LORD weighs the *spirits* (*ruwach*).

Ecclesiastes 3:21 – Who knows the *spirit* (*ruwach*) of the sons of men, which goes upward, and the *spirit* (*ruwach*) of the animal, which goes down to the earth?

Zechariah 12:1 – The burden of the word of the LORD against Israel. Thus says the LORD, who stretches out the heavens, lays the foundation of the earth, and forms the *spirit* (*ruwach*) of man within him.

Several other passages seem to differentiate between the *nephesh* (the soulish part of life) and the *ruwach* (as the mental/intellectual part of life).

Genesis 26:35 – And they were a grief of *mind* (*ruwach*) to Isaac and Rebekah.

Ezekiel 11:5 – Then the Spirit of the LORD fell upon me, and said to me, "Speak! 'Thus says the LORD: "Thus you have said, O house of Israel; for I know the things that come into your *mind* (*ruwach*).""'

Ezekiel 20:32 – What you have in your *mind* (*ruwach*) shall never be, when you say, "We will be like the Gentiles, like the families in other countries, serving wood and stone."

Habakkuk 1:11 – Then his *mind* (*ruwach*) changes, and he transgresses; He commits offense, Ascribing this power to his god.

Life Summarized

There are several key elements to life that distinguish it from all of the other molecular forms and compounds of earth. To begin with, although "earth" was created along with time and the heavens on Day One, the making and shaping of that which was created did not require another *bārā'* (creation) until Day Five. On that day, after the earth and the universe had been prepared in such a way that environment, time references, and food sources were available and fully functioning, God created:

- Life itself – *CHAY*

  - Self-contained, independently functioning, reproducing "kinds" of "living" creatures.

- Things that MOVE

  - Self-directed, independent movement

- Things that have BLOOD

  - Blood is the source for life

- Soul – *NEPHESH*

  - Self-aware, feeling, emotively responding

- Spirit – *RUWACH*

  - Mental consciousness, intuition, instinct

In none of the hundreds of biblical passages that deal with living creatures are plants ever declared or compared to that which God created to carry His life-force. Plants were made from the raw dirt of Day One, and were specifically designed to be for "food" for that "life" that was created on Day Five and Day Six.

CHAPTER SIX
THE BEGINNING
OF LIVING CREATURES

Day Five and Day Six of the creation week bring into existence all of the myriad forms of living creatures. They are brought into existence "abundantly" and are created with the "life" that was discussed in the previous chapter.

There is absolutely no indication in the text of Scripture or in the observational experience of humanity that these creatures were gradually developed over eons of time from some simple "common ancestor." Everything that we know, everything that we observe, everything for which we can devise a test, demonstrates that life "sprang" into existence just as we see it today.

Even in the awful record of the fossils, vast graveyards of creatures buried in continent-wide mudflows catastrophically deposited on scales that defy our imaginations. From the tiny marine invertebrates to the huge bones of extinct "terrible lizards," all appear suddenly and fully formed, appropriately structured to fit their "kind"— just as Scripture insists. Despite the contrary voices of the many who would deny the authority and accuracy of God's revelation, there is absolutely no *scientific* reason to reject the record that God gave us of His unique work of creation.

The Fifth Day

> Then God said, "Let the waters abound with an abundance of living creatures, and let birds fly above the earth across the face of the firmament of the heavens." So God created great sea creatures and every living thing that moves, with which the waters abounded, according to their kind, and every winged bird according to its kind. And God saw that it was good. And God blessed them, saying, "Be fruitful and multiply, and fill the waters in the seas, and let birds multiply on the earth." So the evening and the morning were the fifth day. (Genesis 1:20-23)

The active verb in this passage is *bārā'* or "create." As discussed in detail in the previous chapter, life is much greater than merely a collection of complex molecules. Up until this moment in time, God had been organizing and structuring the "heavens and the earth" so that the entire cosmos would be sufficient to sustain the life that He would "create" on Day Five and Day Six.

As a reminder, the text of Genesis 1 uses the verb *bārā'* only on Day One, Day Five, and Day Six. Days Two, Three, and Four are days of organizing and structuring, along with the specialized "sprouting" of the earth-dirt on Day Three. Apparently, God also "formed" the bodies of the air and land creatures as He gave personal attention to the various "kinds" of living animals that would reveal to us something about Him over the millennia to come.

> Genesis 2:19 – Out of the ground the LORD God formed every beast of the field and every bird of the air, and brought them to Adam to see what he would call them.

> Job 12:7 – But ask now the beasts, and they will teach you; and the birds of the air, and they will tell you.

Whatever God did and however God "made" and "formed" the animals on Days Five and Six, He made sure that we would understand that "creation" was the difference between the living creatures and the food that "sprouted" for them to eat. These creatures were alive!

Designed to fly

All of us have marveled at the birds of our world. Some are exquisite in brilliant color, some sing so wonderfully that our hearts weep with joy, others swarm and pirouette in the air like the most graceful of acrobats and ballet dancers. Every child has watched (and wished for) the freedom of a bird's flight—soaring hither and yon with apparent ease and little thought for the "specks" of life below. The lure of flight has driven many to experiment—from the pathetic Icarus of Greek mythology to the success of the Wright brothers. Flight has no doubt enamored and mystified humanity since Day Six!

Yet all of our engineering skill, fighter jets, rockets, and commercial aircraft fail miserably to mimic the efficient and effective design of the tiniest bird.

Feathers

Wikipedia suggests that feathers are a "complex evolutionary novelty." In other words, there is no legitimate evolutionary story that can account for feathers.

Feathers are not simple parts of flying creatures. They vary in type and use from the soft inner down to the varied wing, tail, and head crests. Feathers have shafts and veins and barrels. They have colored pigments as well as various types of built-in prism designs that refract light. The colors vary all over the spectrum, from plain black and white, to the spectacular radiance that brings an involuntary gasp of breath at its stunning beauty.

False reports of feathered dinosaurs to the contrary, only birds have feathers. Yes, there are flightless birds with feathers (penguins, ostriches, etc.), but they are still birds. No evolutionist has a clue how feathers could have begun to develop. Indeed, there have been countless papers written on how such a thing *might have* come about, but none with observational, empirical data. Most naturalists attribute the origin of feathers to "natural selection," and they explain this process using magic words like: "arose," "emerged," "appeared," "gave rise to...," "derived," "modified," "the early results of...," "burst onto the scene," "manufactured itself," "on the way to becoming...," "evolution drove," "derived emergent properties," and my favorite, "lucky."

Feathers are marvelously designed components for birds. There is no evidence that they evolved from anything else. Everything we know and observe is that feathers were designed to do the functions that they fulfill. Nothing in the observable world gives us any evidence of "developing" feathers. Nothing in the fossil record provides evidence of any "skinather" or "featherin," as if skin from a non-bird creature magically develops into feathers to make that creature a bird. There are no appendages sticking out of any kind of fossil that shows some creature's skin developing sticks that turn into quills that turn into feathers. Nothing.

Feathers came into existence at the same time birds did. God created birds to fly!

Functions

Yes, there were some flying reptiles (now extinct) like the pterosaur and *Pteranodon*—and there are bats (mammals), neither of which have feathers, but they are obviously designed for flying. Since they spend much of their life flying (not walking on the ground), both their bones and their lungs are different.

All flying creatures are built around a skeleton that is both light and composed mostly of hollow bones. This is very different from animals that are designed to walk on solid ground. These flying animals (birds, flying reptiles, bats) were *specifically designed* to fly. Their structure is different. Their activity is different. Their lifestyle is different. The question arises (much like the chicken and the egg question): Were they designed to fly in the first place, or did they develop over time from other walking, crawling, swimming creatures?

The sternum (breastbone) of flying creatures is designed like the keel of a boat. This is the anchor point where most of the flight muscles are attached. Other air-breathing animals have nothing like this. In fact, things that fly have fewer bones than other mammals or reptiles—many of their bones are fused, making the overall skeleton rigid (sort of like the "unibody" of modern automobiles).

Neck vertebrae are different in flying animals than most other animals. Anyone who has ever watched a bird groom its feathers will understand why. Most flying creatures have to keep up the maintenance on their wings and bodies and need these very flexible necks. They don't have hands to help them maintain themselves. Even the "wishbone" that we save at holiday dinners is unique to creatures that fly. Those ridged bones, keel-like sternum, and fused wishbone seem to have a clear purpose to help them fly.

The lungs of flying creatures are very different. Those of us who walk around on the surface of the earth have lungs that act like bellows, pumping air in and out; our whole muscle and skeleton design is built around that function. In fact, we mix the "bad" air with the "good" air in our lungs—mainly because we don't require as much oxygen for our normal functions (walking and sitting, etc.).

Birds, however, have lungs that are like tubes. These air sacs take in air at one end and expel it at the other (sort of like the grill to muffler system of a modern car). Flying lungs are designed to take a unidirectional flow of air as the animal is flying through the air. That design allows for a higher oxygen absorption by the blood when the muscles are working their hardest during flight.

The evidence demonstrates that these flying creatures were designed to fly. Everything that we observe (both in current fauna and in fossils) supports the conclusion that they were "created" as flying creatures, just as Genesis teaches.

Designed to swim

Water-based life is the only category singled out for survival (by omission) from the great judgment of the global Flood "by which the world that then existed perished" (2 Peter 3:6). Evidently, when God "created" the air and water creatures on Day Five, He paid some particular attention to an "abundance" of life that would "fill the waters in the seas" (Genesis 1:22).

Much of what we call "life" lives in the oceans, lakes, and rivers of our planet. Marine biology is a separate discipline with an entire degree program designed for that study in universities. Most of us know that the oceans cover over 70 percent of earth's surface, but what is often not understood is that the habitable volume for sea life is nearly 300 times more than the area that is available for land animals. Some oceans and lakes are actually very deep!

There are approximately 30,000 different species of land animals. That's about the same number as the diverse species of fish. But when you add in the rest of the various water-based living things, the number jumps to well over 200,000. Those water creatures plus the nearly 10,000 species of birds make Day Five a really busy day. God was not using hyperbole when He said: "Let the waters abound with an abundance of living creatures" (Genesis 1:20).

Gills

Talk about different! The capture of necessary oxygen under water is a very different process from that of either birds (tube-like lungs) or land animals (bellow-like lungs). Fish (and many invertebrates, like clams) "rake" in oxygen from water flowing through gills. When a fish (or a clam) opens its mouth, it sucks water (and some goop) into and past a system of filters that sift out the goop. Once past these filters, the water (now purified) passes over the gills.

Gills are amazing, multifaceted devices! The boney pieces that hang in the middle of the mouth support very thin filaments, called *lamellae*. These rows of disk-like lamellae collect the oxygen. Within the lamellae are numerous capillaries that exchange the oxygen for carbon dioxide, allowing the fish (and clams) to breathe. The oxygen goes into the blood stream and the carbon dioxide goes back out into the water. Clever, yes?

Actually, this is not only clever, but absolutely necessary. Water contains less than 5 percent of the oxygen that is available in "air," so these gills have to work more efficiently. Scientists have discovered that gills are able to get about 85 percent of the available oxygen out of the water as it flows through and over these wonderful organs. That 85 percent is much better than humans can do with our lungs. Furthermore, if we had gills like fish, we could not survive on land. Gills require the buoyancy of water to function.

Many water creatures don't have gills. Starfish don't have gills; they breathe through their feet and through small breathing tubes distributed all over their body. Marine worms (there are lots of them) don't have gills and don't have breathing tubes. They breathe through their skin. But everything that lives most of its life in the water is designed to function in the water—with just the right equipment to make their life work. Even the air-breathing aquatic mammals—like whales and porpoises and seals and walruses—have specialized nostrils, lungs, muscles, and other equipment to function best in the water.

It's hard to imagine how any of these creatures could have just "happened."

Scales, skin, and crusty stuff

The oceans, lakes, and rivers of our world are full of amazingly different forms of life. Just as the gills, specialized noses, and various forms of oxygen-gathering organs differ widely by body type, environment, and lifestyle, so do the outer coverings. Scales are common enough, but there is a vast difference among scaly creatures.

Some scales are really big (2 to 3 inches each). Some are microscopic and feel like slick skin—but they are still scales. There are scales made out of bone, scales made out of dentition, and scales made out of cartilage. Some scales have razor sharp ridges down the center or on the sides. Others are flat or curved or rounded or elongated. There are lots of different kinds of scales.

But not everything living in the water has scales. Many creatures have skin. The octopus, squid, and cuttlefish are some of the more commonly known marine creatures with skin. Others, like eels and lampreys, are less known specifically, but wild stories abound about their terrible teeth. Then there are the *Batoidea* (which includes electric rays, butterfly rays, round rays, manta rays, guitarfish, and sawfish)—nearly 500 different kinds of these flat-bodied, wing-shaped animals—all of which have skin rather than scales.

Some of these skin-covered creatures (like squids and cuttlefish) have *chromatrophores* in their skin that enable them to change colors quickly (like a chameleon) to mimic their environmental surroundings. Most of the time the color changes vary to blend in from side-to-side and top-to-bottom, making the animal nearly invisible from every viewpoint. Sometimes these color patterns are flashed back and forth in mating dances.

This color changing ability is fascinating to watch, but the mechanics of making it happen are amazing! Groups of red, yellow, brown, and black pigments are perched above a layer of reflective cells that actually can be oriented in different directions to refract light into different colors. Coordinated muscles "squish" the cells in just the right sequence to produce the right combination of colors that match the surrounding area. The pigments and the refraction capabilities are coupled, sometimes, with chemical reactions that product, essentially, an infinite spectrum of colors—roughly the equivalent of 360 dots per square inch (dpi) on a TV screen or a printed page.

There are numerous evolutionary explanations about how this remarkable ability came about, but those stories make Disney Imagineering look like kids drawing stick men. The biblical record makes a much more believable story. The observable facts demonstrate that these remarkable animals were "created" that way.

And what about the thousands of water life forms that have external skeletons? No scales, no skin, just hard crusty stuff on the outside. How did that just happen? These are not simple creatures. Extinct trilobites and extant sea cucumbers are very different, yet very complex. The marine invertebrates compose the supposed "Cambrian Explosion" that "suddenly" appeared in the fossil record. Starfish, jellyfish, coral, trilobites, worms, cucumbers, etc., just "appeared"—fully formed, just like they are today. And except for the extinct forms, which also appeared in the fossil record fully formed, they all perfectly fit and happily function in their environments—as though they were designed to be there.

Sea monsters

In Genesis 1:21, the King James Version of the Bible translates the Hebrew word *tanniym* with the English word "whales." That leaves an unfortunate misunderstanding in the reader's mind, since the word is elsewhere translated "dragon" or "serpent" or "monster," as it should be.

The fossil record has some rather startling bones of huge marine dinosaurs, most of which appear to be extinct. Several types of extinct plesiosaur are known. An elasmosaur (long neck) and a kronosaur—both are about 50 feet long and are among the more famous. Their fossil bones fit the description of "sea monster" pretty well. Then there are mosasaurs, which range in size from 10 to 50 feet. The Institute for Creation Research has in its collection a skull of a mosasaur found in Morocco that is about 4.5 feet long and nearly 3 feet wide. The skull has segregated jaws and double rows of teeth. Sea monster indeed!

Any one of these fossils could have been the dead ancestor of the living Leviathan that God Himself describes to Job during the discourse between God and Job recorded in chapters 38 through 41. One land dinosaur and one marine dinosaur were certainly alive at the time of Job—who was a contemporary of Abraham. Notice God's description of the "sea monster."

> "Can you draw out Leviathan with a hook, Or snare his tongue with a line which you lower? Can you put a reed through his nose, Or pierce his jaw with a hook? Will he make many supplications to you?
>
> "Will he speak softly to you? Will he make a covenant

with you? Will you take him as a servant forever? Will you play with him as with a bird, Or will you leash him for your maidens? Will your companions make a banquet of him? Will they apportion him among the merchants?

"Can you fill his skin with harpoons, Or his head with fishing spears? Lay your hand on him; Remember the battle—Never do it again!

"Indeed, any hope of overcoming him is false; Shall one not be overwhelmed at the sight of him? No one is so fierce that he would dare stir him up.

"Who then is able to stand against Me? Who has preceded Me, that I should pay him? Everything under heaven is Mine.

"I will not conceal his limbs, His mighty power, or his graceful proportions. Who can remove his outer coat? Who can approach him with a double bridle? Who can open the doors of his face, With his terrible teeth all around? His rows of scales are his pride, Shut up tightly as with a seal; One is so near another That no air can come between them; They are joined one to another, They stick together and cannot be parted.

"His sneezings flash forth light, And his eyes are like the eyelids of the morning. Out of his mouth go burning lights; Sparks of fire shoot out. Smoke goes out of his nostrils, As from a boiling pot and burning rushes. His breath kindles coals, And a flame goes out of his mouth.

"Strength dwells in his neck, And sorrow dances before him. The folds of his flesh are joined together; They are firm on him and cannot be moved. His heart is as hard as stone, Even as hard as the lower millstone. When he raises himself up, the mighty are afraid; Because of his crashings they are beside themselves.

"Though the sword reaches him, it cannot avail; Nor

does spear, dart, or javelin. He regards iron as straw, And bronze as rotten wood. The arrow cannot make him flee; Slingstones become like stubble to him. Darts are regarded as straw; He laughs at the threat of javelins. His undersides are like sharp potsherds; He spreads pointed marks in the mire.

"He makes the deep boil like a pot; He makes the sea like a pot of ointment. He leaves a shining wake behind him; One would think the deep had white hair.

"On earth there is nothing like him, Which is made without fear. He beholds every high thing; He is king over all the children of pride." (Job 41:1-34)

Now we do have a problem. Either God is confused about what He created or the modern scholars are right and this creature is nothing more than a crocodile. The words of the biblical text do not describe a crocodile. Anyone who can read would see that. The awesome marine creature described by God to Job is much different from any animal about which we have current knowledge.

It is remarkable that every culture, from just about every recorded time era, has stories about sea monsters. Yes, some of them are pretty wild, but as recently as 1934 several newspapers recorded the finding of a 30-foot-long "sea monster" washed up on the beach south of Henry Island in British Columbia. A Japanese sea trawler caught a long-dead sea creature in its nets off the coast of New Zealand in 1974. That "thing" looked suspiciously like a plesiosaur, although it was too decayed to make any kind of a positive identification. And surely the news and speculation about creatures like the "Loch Ness monster" have not escaped notice. While these stories do not prove the existence of sea monsters, there are similarities that run through many of these accounts in history that often match elements of what God described to Job.

Everywhere one can look, from the soaring birds and scary pterodactyls, from the sea monster to the sea cucumber, the design, purpose, complex construction, environmental fit, awesome beauty and instant camouflage of these creatures all display and demonstrate the majestic wonder of God's fifth day of creation.

"And God saw that it was good."

The Sixth Day

Continuing to create and make the living creatures, God now turns His attention to the land.

> Then God said, "Let the earth bring forth the living creature according to its kind: cattle and creeping thing and beast of the earth, each according to its kind"; and it was so. And God made the beast of the earth according to its kind, cattle according to its kind, and everything that creeps on the earth according to its kind. And God saw that it was good. (Genesis 1:24-25)

Cattle

This descriptive term (Hebrew *behemah*) is used by the Creator and later by Moses to describe the land animals that people were most familiar with. "Cattle" is a general term still used to mean any kind of livestock from cows to sheep. Most of the 189 times the term appears in the Hebrew text, the context is referencing food or sacrificial laws (Exodus through Deuteronomy). Obviously, the reference to food was made long *after* permission was given to Noah to eat animal flesh (Genesis 9:3).

Whatever these animals were, it appears clear that they would have included all of the land animals that mankind has generally domesticated or raised agriculturally for food. The main difference between these "cattle" and the "beasts of the earth" seems to be their personality preference. Yes, as discussed earlier in the chapter on life, animals have both a "soul" and a "spirit" and do express self-awareness as well as distinct personalities. Some, of course, are less personable than others, but there is an obvious gap between farm animals and house pets and the "wild beasts" of our planet.

Just what separates the "fowls" that fly in the atmosphere of Day Five (most of which feed and house on land) and the "cattle" of Day Six is not clear either in biology or in Scripture. God separated them in His mind, however, and as any person who has had close contact with animals knows, farm animals and house pets are given far more freedom than birds. Cows and horses respond to their keepers (we don't own anything that God created) in a much more free and friendly manner than do birds.

Something about the way that God made these "cattle" is different from the way He made the birds that "fly above the earth across the face of the firmament of the heavens" (Genesis 1:20). Anyone who has kept a parakeet, a canary, a macaw, or a finch knows this: Birds need a cage or a chain or they will fly away. Cats and dogs, however, know the hand that feeds them and often "manage" the people who care for them! Whatever the difference, it is profound how God made these creatures distinct and the "kind" of animals He made on separate days.

Creeping things

Here is a second broad term used by the Creator to designate a category of animals that is different from "cattle." The Hebrew word is *remes,* and is used mostly in the creation record, the account of the global Flood, and the dietary laws. Twice the word appears in the Psalms, and once in a prophetic passage. All of the occasions appear to speak of smaller animals that "slink" or "glide" in the more inaccessible parts of the earth.

The man-made system of taxonomy, as useful as it may be for our efforts to categorize, doesn't seem to apply. God uses a much broader concept—evidently creating the vast "kinds" in direct proportion to how these creatures would relate to human interaction. Thus, "cattle" would be the types of animals that would be more easily brought into association with man. "Creeping things" and "beasts of the earth" are broad summaries of animal life that would not normally be part of a domesticated household.

Therefore, it seems appropriate to think of these "creeping things" as the weasels, rodents, possums, shrews, reptiles, amphibians, etc. That list is in no sense meant to be complete, but merely illustrative, since there are nearly 20,000 different species of those kinds of "creeping things." The list would probably also include the 1,000,000 or so species of insects and the 100,000 or so species of spiders and scorpions. People don't generally get along with any of those.

Beasts of the earth

This final category obviously includes everything that is not "cattle" or "creeping thing." That phrase appears 24 times in the Old Testament. Most of the places where the phrase appears outside of the creation passage, it is used to describe the beasts eating the other animals—and in some cases the flesh of wicked men. Whatever these animals are, they are not pets!

When God gives His discourse to Job, He mentions the "lion," the "wild goat," the "wild ass," and the "ostrich" as samples of the types of animals that were known to Job, but not animals that Job or his fellow men would keep around their house or their fields. God also takes special care to describe "behemoth" and "leviathan"—both of which are huge, wild animals about which Job was familiar, but which Job would not plan to keep as pets.

Leviathan is obviously a "sea monster" that, fortunately, has become extinct. Behemoth fits perfectly the description of the larger sauropods (four-footed dinosaurs) that we find in the fossil record.

"Look now at the behemoth, which I made along with you; He eats grass like an ox. See now, his strength is in his hips, And his power is in his stomach muscles.

"He moves his tail like a cedar; The sinews of his thighs are tightly knit. His bones are like beams of bronze, His ribs like bars of iron.

"He is the first of the ways of God; Only He who made him can bring near His sword.

"Surely the mountains yield food for him, And all the beasts of the field play there. He lies under the lotus trees, In a covert of reeds and marsh. The lotus trees cover him with their shade; The willows by the brook surround him. Indeed the river may rage, Yet he is not disturbed; He is confident, though the Jordan gushes into his mouth, Though he takes it in his eyes, Or one pierces his nose with a snare." (Job 40:15-24)

Many of the modern Bible editions attempt to pass off this creature as either an elephant or a hippopotamus. Once again, either God was confused about what He and Job were familiar with, or the scholars are wrong. Neither an elephant nor a hippopotamus has a tail, for instance, that resembles a cedar tree. And although the hippopotamus lives in a river, the elephant does not. An elephant may live near mountains and under trees, but the hippopotamus does not. The total description is easily matched to what we know from the fossil record.

It seems that God is using examples of the "beasts of the earth" to help Job see that there is much that he does not know—and that God alone is both Creator and Caretaker of the "wild" beasts.

After its kind

There is not much to add to the discussion in chapter three of this book about the command from the Creator to all replicating processes. All of them, from the simplest plant to the most complex life, were limited to reproducing "after its kind." This emphasis is repeated on Day Three to the "sprouts" of earth, and on Day Five and Day Six to all of the living creatures. Everything was to "fill the earth" and be "fruitful"—but only "after its kind."

The design implications are vital to understand. Not only do the obvious limitations prohibit the atheistic concept of a "common ancestor," but also the inferences that certainly seem to be verified by our observation. That is, within each "kind" is the design power to adapt quickly to environmental changes that will permit the "kind" to propagate itself over time.

Human efforts to categorize differences between species are just that—human effort. Mankind is just now scratching the surface of the enormously complex DNA instructions that reside in the "seed" of everything that reproduces. As more is unraveled (literally) and more is documented, scholars are becoming aware that the so-called "junk DNA" is now clearly *not* junk! Perhaps we will never fully understand what our Creator produced in the "seed" of plants and animals. But what all scholars are beginning to understand better is that "nature" doesn't "select" anything.

The power to adapt resides within the organism.

The Image of God

> Then God said, "Let Us make man in Our image, according to Our likeness; let them have dominion over the fish of the sea, over the birds of the air, and over the cattle, over all the earth and over every creeping thing that creeps on the earth." So God created man in His own image; in the image of God He created him; male and female He created them. Then God blessed them, and God said to them, "Be fruitful and multiply; fill the earth and subdue it; have dominion over the fish of the sea, over the birds of the air, and over every living thing that moves on the earth." (Genesis 1:26-28)

Theologians and students of Scripture have been pondering this passage since it was recorded. Just what is it that God "created" in His own "image"? Just what *is* God's image? There are a number of hints in the Bible, but not enough to be completely sure; some things remain secret with God (Deuteronomy 29:29). Here are a few of the special characteristics of man that are unique to humanity.

Only one of each

When the Creator came to the time on Day Six when He determined to "make" man, He made only one male and one female body. All of the other living animals in the air, in the water, on and under the earth, were made at least in the hundreds of pairs, if not thousands or millions. They were "abundant" and "filled" the air and sea and land.

Not so with Adam and Eve.

> And the LORD God formed man of the dust of the ground, and breathed into his nostrils the breath of life; and man became a living being. (Genesis 2:7)

> And the LORD God caused a deep sleep to fall on Adam, and he slept; and He took one of his ribs, and closed up the flesh in its place. Then the rib which the LORD God had taken from man He made into a woman, and He brought her to the man. (Genesis 2:21-22)

Genesis 2 has a definite place in the creation narrative and will be discussed below. But please notice the precise language used about the "forming" of Adam and the "making" of Eve. The Holy Spirit specifically used the Hebrew word *yatsar* to describe what God did to bring about the complete body of Adam. As was discussed in chapter two of this book, *yatsar* is a "hands-on" verb used to describe personal involvement like an artist painting a picture or a sculptor developing a figure. This was the "first man" (1 Corinthians 15:47) and was unique from everything else that had been made.

Then, in complete harmony with the later revealed plan for the relationship between male and female, the Creator took some "rib" from Adam and "made" a woman. The English translations don't quite do justice to the record. *Tesla* is the Hebrew word used and every other time it appears in the Bible it is translated "side." Surely what God took from Adam would have included a rib, but there was muscle and other tissue as well, which is why Adam later said: "This is now bone of my bones and flesh of my flesh; She shall be called Woman, Because she was taken out of Man" (Genesis 2:23).

In both cases, with the handful of dirt and the piece of Adam's side, God "formed" and "made" the independent and unique bodies of Adam and Eve.

A temple for God

There are several related pieces of biblical data that need to be considered. Here are some of the more obvious concepts that we can connect.

Jesus Christ is the visible form of God

And the Word became flesh and dwelt among us, and we beheld His glory, the glory as of the only begotten of the Father, full of grace and truth. (John 1:14)

"I and My Father are one." (John 10:30)

Jesus said to him, "…He who has seen Me has seen the Father." (John 14:9)

For it pleased the Father that in Him all the fullness should dwell. (Colossians 1:19)

For in Him dwells all the fullness of the Godhead bodily. (Colossians 2:9)

Jesus Christ has always appeared in human form

Abraham: …three men were standing by him (Genesis 18:2)…And the LORD said, "Shall I hide from Abraham what I am doing" (Genesis 18:17)…So the LORD went His way as soon as He had finished speaking with Abraham; and Abraham returned to his place. Now the two angels came to Sodom in the evening. (Genesis 18:33-19:1)

Jacob: Then Jacob was left alone; and a Man wrestled with him until the breaking of day….And Jacob called the name of the place Peniel: "For I have seen God face to face, and my life is preserved." (Genesis 32:24, 30)

Joshua: …when Joshua was by Jericho, that he lifted his eyes and looked, and behold, a Man stood opposite him with His sword drawn in His hand. And Joshua went to Him and said to Him, "Are You for us or for our adversar-

ies?" So He said, "No, but as Commander of the army of the LORD I have now come." (Joshua 5:13-14)

Daniel: I was watching in the night visions, And behold, One like the Son of Man, Coming with the clouds of heaven! (Daniel 7:13)

Peter, James, John: Jesus …led them up on a high mountain by themselves; and He was transfigured before them. His face shone like the sun, and His clothes became as white as the light. (Matthew 17:1-2)

Apostle John: …and in the midst of the seven lampstands One like the Son of Man, clothed with a garment down to the feet and girded about the chest with a golden band. (Revelation 1:13)…Then I looked, and behold, a white cloud, and on the cloud sat One like the Son of Man, having on His head a golden crown, and in His hand a sharp sickle. (Revelation 14:14)

Jesus Christ was slain before the foundation of the world

…the Lamb slain from the foundation of the world. (Revelation 13:8)

He indeed was foreordained before the foundation of the world, but was manifest in these last times for you. (1 Peter 1:20)

A body You have prepared for Me. (Hebrews 10:5)

We shall be like Him

One of the great mysteries of eternity is the vast changes that will be brought about to those who are born again when they join the Lord Jesus after the resurrection.

So also is the resurrection of the dead. The body is sown in corruption, it is raised in incorruption. It is sown in dishonor, it is raised in glory. It is sown in weakness, it is raised in power. It is sown a natural body, it is raised a spiritual body. There is a natural body, and there is a spiritual body. (1 Corinthians 15:42-44)

And as we have borne the image of the man of dust, we shall also bear the image of the heavenly Man. Now this I say, brethren, that flesh and blood cannot inherit the kingdom of God; nor does corruption inherit incorruption. Behold, I tell you a mystery: We shall not all sleep, but we shall all be changed—in a moment, in the twinkling of an eye, at the last trumpet. For the trumpet will sound, and the dead will be raised incorruptible, and we shall be changed. For this corruptible must put on incorruption, and this mortal must put on immortality. (1 Corinthians 15:49-53)

Beloved, now we are children of God; and it has not yet been revealed what we shall be, but we know that when He is revealed, we shall be like Him, for we shall see Him as He is. (1 John 3:2)

Obviously, these contrasts between the "earthly" and the "heavenly" reflect the awful judgment of Genesis 3, when everything in the "whole creation" (Romans 8:22) began to fall apart and Adam and Eve suddenly "knew they were naked." More on this as the issues of sin and death are discussed in chapter eight.

What is of consequence here as far as the "image" of God in man is concerned, however, is the clear acknowledgement in Scripture that our earthly bodies now do not "fit" the requirements for the "new heaven and the new earth." What we possess now will be "changed" before we can be "as he is" during eternity. The face-to-face fellowship that Adam and Eve knew in the Garden prior to their rebellion (Genesis 1:29; 2:8, 16; 3:8-10) was taken away, and the relationship between the Creator and His crowning creation needed to be reconciled.

Everything that the Bible tells us about the age-long salvation effort on the part of God toward man is that after we have been "drawn" to the Father (John 6:44) and given the faith to believe in what has been done by the Lord Jesus on our behalf (Ephesians 2:8-9), we are a "new man which was created according to God, in true righteousness and holiness" (Ephesians 4:24). Something about what Adam and Eve possessed at creation, before their fall, is restored at the moment of the new birth. That "something" was at least part of the "image" of God. That "something" may well have been the "eternal" and "spiritual" part of humanity that we *do not* possess prior to salvation.

Three Important Points

All of these varied and scattered indicators throughout Scripture seem to highlight three very important points about the "image" of God that was "created" in both male and female on Day Six of the creation week.

- One: There *was* an eternal part to us that no longer exists, and won't until we are given "eternal life" at the point of salvation. Apparently, Adam and Eve possessed that quality when they were created.

- Two: The human body form is directly connected with the incarnation of our Lord Jesus, as indicated throughout Scripture, both in His appearances prior to His entry into this world and after His resurrection.

- Three: The mortal body that humanity is now born into after the terrible curse rendered in Genesis 3 must be "changed" into a suitable "immortal" body that will be compatible with the eternal body of the Lord Jesus.

Whatever God did for Adam and Eve that made them "in His image," He did not do for the entirety of the rest of creation. As marvelous as the many life forms, shapes, functions, and reflections about Gods attributes, none of the sea, air, or land creatures can "fellowship" with the Creator—only man. Indeed, one day every tongue in the universe will confess the Lordship of Jesus Christ in an open assembly around the Throne in heaven. Now, however, mankind alone is afforded the opportunity to be "redeemed" and "reconciled" to the great Creator.

The "image" that was rendered "dead in trespasses and sins" (Ephesians 2:1) because of the horrible rebellion of Adam, now is given the opportunity to receive the "guarantee of our inheritance until the redemption of the purchased possession" (Ephesians 1:14) "for salvation ready to be revealed in the last time" (1 Peter 1:5). Man alone can be born again.

> ...to a living hope through the resurrection of Jesus Christ from the dead, to an inheritance incorruptible and undefiled and that does not fade away, reserved in heaven for you, who are kept by the power of God through faith for salvation ready to be revealed in the last time. (1 Peter 1:3-5)

CHAPTER SEVEN
THE BEGINNING OF
HUMAN RESPONSIBILITY

In the previous two chapters, our discussion has focused on the vast differences between the various "kinds" of flora and fauna that God created on earth. Several issues should be clear from the biblical information.

Quick Review

Plants were made on Day Three from the basic components of the planet and were designed by the Creator to be "food" for the living creatures that would follow on Day Five and Day Six. Although complex molecular structures were involved, none of these earth "sprouts" were living beings. None of the characteristics of living beings are ever ascribed to plants.

Plants were, however, the first complex structures designed by God to reproduce—to have "seed in itself." What we now know of DNA is that it contains the enormously complex information that enables the qualities of the various "kinds" of plants to reproduce—but "after its kind." There is absolutely no hint in any part of the biblical data that these complex structures "developed" over ages; rather they were immediately generated at the command of the Creator to "sprout." Nothing in the Bible suggests long ages of naturalistic and/ or evolutionary innovation.

Life in the water and air

Life itself was "created" on Day Five in the form of air and water creatures. These "abundant" creatures were to "fill" the water and the "heaven" with their vast variety and to be a part of what David calls the daily "speech" and nightly "knowledge" that goes into the entire world (Psalm 19:1-4). The unique features of those creatures that were designed to live and function in water are so different from those that were designed to live and function in air, that no reasonable evaluation would conclude that an "evolution" occurred—except those who do not want to entertain the idea of an omnipotent and omniscient Creator.

It is on Day Five that we have enumerated the unique qualities of living beings. Indeed, the very word "life" is never used to define plants. All living things have the ability of independent movement, self-conscious awareness, emotive personalities, and intellectual prowess to varying degrees. None of these characterizes are ever applied to the food of Day Three.

Life on the land

The land creatures that were brought into existence on Day Six were also very different from the sea and air creatures of Day Five, yet all shared in the "living" nature that God had created. Each creature provides some insight to the nature and character of their Creator, adding more evidence of the infinite capabilities of the One who brought them into existence.

Variations in personalities became more obvious in the creatures of the land. The "cattle" were more easily domesticated by man and shared an affinity to environments more clearly under the control of man. "Beasts of the earth" and "creeping things," while magnificent and beautiful, were less likely to be compatible with man and tended to be more content in their own environments—demonstrating once again the specificity of design so clearly observable today.

Life of man

Man was and is unique. Not only was Adam "formed" by the personal touch of the Creator Himself, and Eve made from the very bone and flesh of Adam, but God only made one each! In contrast, thousands if not millions of animals were made; all of the references to the other living creatures were written in the plural: bird<u>s</u>, great sea creature<u>s</u>, cattle, creeping thing<u>s</u>, beast<u>s</u> of the earth. There was to be "an abundance of living creatures" (Genesis 1:20).

The one man and the one woman—each of whom was specially "created" in God's own image—were vastly different from the rest of the living creatures of our planet.

While we share the "life" of other living animals, our bodies are enormously more versatile and capable than other living things. Human emotion expresses a vast range of feelings and reactions that no animal shares. Intellectually, the human brain far exceeds any animal brain in capacity and ability. While all creation will one day acknowledge the Creator, it is only man who now joyfully worships, or consciously rebels.

Contrasting Worldviews

Perhaps it is also worth reviewing the contrast between the two opposite worldviews that dominate the thinking and educational processes of humanity. The view that has been revealed to us from the Creator is essentially expressed in and throughout the Bible. In contrast, the alternative worldview is essentially atheistic, rejecting the possibility of an omniscient and omnipotent Being.

The biblical worldview is most referred to as a "creationist" worldview.

The atheistic worldview is most presented as an evolutionary or naturalistic worldview.

Biblical-Creationist Worldview	Atheistic-Naturalistic Worldview
Man created in the image of God	Man is the result of random, blind chance
Man is priceless and eternal	Man is purposeless and temporal
Each person is an irreplaceable, unique creation of God	Each person is a replaceable chemical organism of chance
Mankind is preserved by his Creator and rules as God's steward	Mankind has survived and become superior to all other forms of life
Life has meaning both now and in eternity	Life is without meaning and ends with death
God exists and is transcendent to all that exists	God does not exist and nothing exists beyond nature and the cosmos
The universe is ordered by God for eternal purposes. Man can depend on that order.	The universe is chaotic and purposeless. Man can never depend on anything in the universe.
Man's chief end is to glorify God and to serve Him forever	Survival and reproduction is the best that man can accomplish

Although there are attempts to hybridize or harmonize these two worldview systems, they are not compatible. Even a cursory evaluation makes this observation clear.

The Genesis Mandate

Then God blessed them, and God said to them, "Be fruitful and multiply; fill the earth and subdue it; have dominion over the fish of the sea, over the birds of the air, and over every living thing that moves on the earth." And God said, "See, I have given you every herb that yields seed which is on the face of all the earth, and every tree whose fruit yields seed; to you it shall be for food. Also, to every beast of the earth, to every bird of the air, and to everything that creeps on the earth, in which there is life, I have given every green herb for food"; and it was so. (Genesis 1:28-30)

There are a number of key terms that must be analyzed in these important verses. Essentially, this text sets the stage for the responsibility that all of humanity would carry as long as earth endures. Adam, as the federal head of human kind, is delegated authority over the creation, both its flora and its fauna. This stewardship has never been withdrawn nor abrogated in any way, except somewhat extended and subrogated to collective humanity after the great Flood during Noah's day.

Be fruitful and multiply

This is the portion of the mandate that most folks remember. However, it appears to be most often interpreted: "Have lots of kids." There really is much more to this command.

Obviously both the terms used and the phrase itself imply reproduction. The same phrase was given to the fish and the birds of Day Five (Genesis 1:22), to all the animals that came off the Ark (Genesis 8:17), as well as to Adam and Eve in the initial mandate and later to Noah and his children after the Flood was over (Genesis 9:1). But if all this command signifies is to "breed" prolifically, then there is not much to it.

It is worthy of note that the plant food of Day Three was *not* given this command—God merely noting that these "sprouts" were to "yield" after their kind. Such an omission would suggest that there is more to being "fruitful" than merely "yielding." Life is both more complicated and more complex than food. Many, many studies have been done on the reproductive habits and mating rituals of living creatures. Some are elaborate, some by forcing others away from the possibilities, some by environmental stimuli, some even by "love at first sight." But whatever is involved, being "fruitful" is not passive!

As one follows the use of this idea throughout Scripture, not only is the concept of choice and selection involved, but a desire to "multiply" in such a way that the future is impacted—even controlled by the "fruit." Consider the promises of God to Abraham.

> Now the LORD had said to Abram... "I will make you a great nation; I will bless you And make your name great; And you shall be a blessing." (Genesis 12:1-2)

> "My covenant is with you, and you shall be a father of many nations. No longer shall your name be called Abram, but your name shall be Abraham; for I have made you a father of many nations." (Genesis 17:4-5)

> "...since Abraham shall surely become a great and mighty nation, and all the nations of the earth shall be blessed in him? For I have known him, in order that he may command his children and his household after him, that they keep the way of the LORD, to do righteousness and justice, that the LORD may bring to Abraham what He has spoken to him." (Genesis 18:18-19)

Much more could be said and many more references cited, but it is clear that God intended for mankind to take the responsibility of "multiplying" far more seriously than merely having lots of children. Whether you agree with the practice or not, fathers have for millennia *chosen* husbands for their daughters—and many societies still practice that custom. Even in the sophisticated Western world, fathers still try to influence the marriages of their children, knowing that there are many, many consequences of raising children and extending families.

And, of course, that pressure to protect and direct the next generation is a God-placed concept in all living creatures—especially among humans. That "instinct" to be fruitful and multiply is the fountainhead from which the rest of the Genesis Mandate flows.

Fill the earth

The Hebrew verb *male'* is broadly used in the nearly 300 times it is found the Old Testament. It is used to describe "filling" a space as when the locusts filled the houses of the Egyptians during the ten plagues (Exodus 10:6). It is sometimes used to identify the completion of a specific time that has elapsed, like when the seven days were "fulfilled" after the Lord turned the Nile into blood (Exodus 7:25) or as when Daniel had "fulfilled" three weeks of fasting (Daniel 10:3). But many of the passages deal with the "completing" or "fulfilling" of promises and prophecies. Frequently the term is used to indicate the completion of those prophecies or to encompass the various stages by which the promise or prophecy was accomplished.

Given the clear application throughout the Scriptures that God Himself is involved in "filling" the earth with the nations under His sovereign plan, it seems that this initial mandate to "fill" may imply more than merely biological reproduction. Consider these passages.

> Acts 17:26 – And He has made from one blood every nation of men to dwell on all the face of the earth, and has determined their preappointed times and the boundaries of their dwellings.

> Deuteronomy 32:8 – When the Most High divided their inheritance to the nations, When He separated the sons of Adam, He set the boundaries of the peoples According to the number of the children of Israel.

> Revelation 17:10 – There are also seven kings. Five have fallen, one is, and the other has not yet come. And when he comes, he must continue a short time.

Whatever may have been delegated to humanity (and to animals) in the authorization to "fill" the earth, it is certainly clear that God has "arranged" (if that is the proper word) for His creation to "fulfill" His plans—even though many (both men and animals) do their best to thwart those plans.

The capacity to "fill" would involve at least the following abilities:

- Frequent and successful reproduction "after its kind"

- Early maturity and long fertility potential

- Informational capacity (DNA) within the "kind" to adapt to new environments

- Intellectual capacity to plan for and protect successful "filling"

- Geometric growth patterns that stabilize generations and communities

All of these elements are clear design features and have nothing to do with the atheistic idea of random, chaotic, purposeless "natural selection" that is the popular magic word of the evolutionary worldview. Everything we see, everything that we know about how living creatures produce and prosper, verifies these basic patterns of life.

Subdue the earth

Now comes the hard part. God asks Adam (and through him all of us) to "conquer" earth. The Hebrew word *kabash* is only used 15 times in the Old Testament, but it always carries the idea of bringing something into or under subjection. Three obvious references will suffice to illustrate the use of the word.

> 2 Samuel 8:11 – King David also dedicated these to the LORD, along with the silver and gold that he had dedicated from all the nations which he had *subdued.*

> Jeremiah 34:16 – Then you turned around and profaned My name, and every one of you brought back his male and female slaves, whom you had set at liberty, at their pleasure, and brought them back into *subjection*, to be your male and female slaves.

> Micah 7:19 – He will again have compassion on us, And will *subdue* our iniquities. You will cast all our sins Into

the depths of the sea.

Obviously, when the Creator issued the authority to Adam and to Eve to "subdue" the earth, God was not giving an order that would be easily carried out. Mankind would have to learn about earth's systems and processes, organize and utilize that knowledge in productive ways to benefit others and honor the Creator, disseminate the information gained and distribute the products to everyone, and receive and detail the divine evaluation ("very good").

Have dominion

Just as "subdue" does not demand misuse of the authority to "conquer" for hurtful purposes, neither does "have dominion" imply rape and plunder. Yes, many individuals and nations have used God's delegated authority to harm others and exploit earth's resources for their own gain. However, violation of purpose does not negate original intent. Evil deeds are judged to be evil because they expose the behavior that is not good. Good is evaluated as that which provides benefit to mankind. Evil is recognized by its selfish and greedy rejection of such benefit.

When the Creator granted the authority to "subdue" (conquer) and to "have dominion" (rule), He had just brought into existence his "image" (man) who would share regency with Him over the beautiful planet in its pristine condition. It is true that those stewards would soon rebel against God's ownership and distort the authority that had been granted (Genesis 3). What has happened subsequent to that rebellion, however, in no way abrogates the design and purpose of His "good" mandate.

The Hebrew word *radah* is used 27 times in the Old Testament, always having the basic meaning of "rule." It can be used in the sense of an evil rule, even a rule with "force and cruelty" (Ezekiel 34:4), but that idea is not inherent in the word. The ruler determines the kind of rule, not the authority itself. The *way* one rules is determined by the character of the one who rules.

The authority to rule comes from the Owner.

> You [the Creator] have made him [man] to have domin-
> ion over the works of Your hands; You have put all things
> under his feet, all sheep and oxen—even the beasts of the
> field, the birds of the air, and the fish of the sea that pass
> through the paths of the seas. O LORD, our Lord, How
> excellent is Your name in all the earth! (Psalm 8:6-9)

Man as Steward

Herein lies the crux of the debate. Just who is the boss? The Bible
is replete with the clear message that God (the Creator) owns everything.

> The earth is the LORD's, and all its fullness, The world and
> those who dwell therein. For He has founded it upon the
> seas, And established it upon the waters. (Psalm 24:1-2)

> Thus says the LORD, The Holy One of Israel....I have
> made the earth, And created man on it. I—My hands—
> stretched out the heavens, and all their host I have com-
> manded. (Isaiah 45:11-12)

> For every beast of the forest is Mine, And the cattle on a
> thousand hills. I know all the birds of the mountains, and
> the wild beasts of the field are Mine. (Psalm 50:10-11)

> The silver is Mine, and the gold is Mine,' says the LORD
> of hosts. (Haggai 2:8)

> Behold, all souls are Mine; The soul of the father As well
> as the soul of the son is Mine. (Ezekiel 18:4)

There is no lack of clarity. Either one accepts the ownership of the
Creator, or it is rejected. The message is not ambiguous. And indeed,
this is the point of the argument. If God is the Creator, then He is my
Owner and I must one day answer to Him how well I have dealt with
what He has given me—including my own life!

If, however, God does not exist (as the evolutionary naturalist would insist) or if He is merely some sort of divine "spark" that left everything else up to nature and to me (as the Deist or Agnostic might propose), then humanity, as the pinnacle of evolutionary development, has the perfect right to make up its own rules and do as it pleases.

The example of the Garden

Everybody knows the story of the Garden of Eden. Fewer have actually read the account, and fewer still have given much thought to what is taught by the event.

When Moses edited the Book of Genesis, it seems clear that he had access to at least eleven source documents from which he complied the entire record. These source documents can be easily recognized by the subscript (much like the closing of a letter) appended to the section of the text that precedes it. The information of the creation week sequence is signed off by the notation: "This is the history of the heavens and the earth when they were created" (Genesis 2:4).

The events detailing the Garden of Eden are recorded by Adam himself. His record covers the moment when he began his existence on the sixth day through the end of his life and is signed: "This is the book of the genealogy of Adam" (Genesis 5:1). Chapter 2 of Genesis contains a rather detailed record of the special "garden" that the Creator had made for Adam, including much about the nature of the land and the location of that garden. The quotation below leaves out some of those geographical and environmental details so that it is possible to concentrate on the initial example of God's delegating authority to "subdue" and "have dominion" over what had been made.

> The LORD God planted a garden eastward in Eden, and there He put the man whom He had formed. And out of the ground the LORD God made every tree grow that is pleasant to the sight and good for food. The tree of life was also in the midst of the garden, and the tree of the knowledge of good and evil.
>
> Then the LORD God took the man and put him in the

garden of Eden to tend and keep it….Out of the ground the LORD God formed every beast of the field and every bird of the air, and brought them to Adam to see what he would call them. And whatever Adam called each living creature, that was its name. So Adam gave names to all cattle, to the birds of the air, and to every beast of the field. But for Adam there was not found a helper comparable to him.

And the LORD God caused a deep sleep to fall on Adam, and he slept; and He took one of his ribs, and closed up the flesh in its place. Then the rib which the LORD God had taken from man He made into a woman, and He brought her to the man. And Adam said: "This is now bone of my bones and flesh of my flesh; She shall be called Woman, Because she was taken out of Man."

On-the-job training

This point is so obvious that we often either overlook it or take the principle for granted. All of our "work" experience—in every culture in every historical context—is enhanced by some form of experiential learning process. Yes, there are "institutions" of higher learning where many are trained in the theory of the role that one may have in the adult world, but everyone who has had to earn a living knows that "entry level" means just that! One starts at the proverbial "bottom of the ladder."

Just so with Adam.

The Garden of the Lord

As Adam writes his *memoirs*, he notes that God "had planted" a Garden toward the east of Eden. Adam was writing this "book" (Genesis 5:1) toward the end of his life, recalling that he had been "placed" in that Garden on the day that he had been created. It is clear from Adam's own recollection that this was before "any plant of the field was in the earth and before any herb of the field had grown"—before

Adam began to cultivate the ground.

Eden was a territory (state, country, locale) in which this Garden was established. Adam lists three other territories: Havilah, Cush, and Assyria. Those names have survived into our era (as have the name of some of the rivers mentioned), but the locations were destroyed with the great cataclysm of the global Flood. Adam records the geographical markers in his "book" for those who would come after him. His "book" was written long after he had been expelled from the Garden because of his rebellion.

The lush beauty of God's garden is remembered by several Bible authors.

> Genesis 13:10 – And Lot lifted his eyes and saw all the plain of Jordan, that it was well watered everywhere (before the LORD destroyed Sodom and Gomorrah) like the garden of the LORD, like the land of Egypt as you go toward Zoar.

> Isaiah 51:3 – For the LORD will comfort Zion…her desert like the garden of the LORD; Joy and gladness will be found in it, Thanksgiving and the voice of melody.

> Ezekiel 28:13 – Thou hast been in Eden the garden of God….(speaking of Lucifer)

> Ezekiel 31:9 – I have made him fair by the multitude of his branches: so that all the trees of Eden, that were in the garden of God

> Joel 2:3 – …the land is as the garden of Eden before them….

This was a grand estate that God Himself had made for Adam, from which Adam was expected to begin the stewardship of the earth. God brought Adam to this place (and all who would eventually come from him) to teach him the lessons of planet management.

The lesson of ownership

The source of many if not most difficulties in all relationships is a clear understanding of responsibilities. In business one must understand (and abide by) the rules of the boss. Good executives seek the advice of their subordinates and provide great latitude for their senior managers—but those who seek to take over the company often find themselves out of a job! Someone has well said: "An organization with two heads is a monster. An organization with no head is dead!"

In marriage, one partner has the final say—or the marriage falls apart. God has established some rules for marriage, by the way, and those marriages that follow those rules survive and thrive. Those that don't, don't. Rebellion often occurs and sometimes seems to be successful, but the disorder that flows and the damage that occurs from such a rebellion continues for a long time.

Thus the lesson of ownership.

It is interesting to note that God "performed" creative acts in the sight of Adam as the first lesson—a lesson that Adam would remember for all of his life.

> And out of the ground the LORD God made every tree grow that is pleasant to the sight and good for food. The tree of life was also in the midst of the garden, and the tree of the knowledge of good and evil. (Genesis 2:9)

These trees were not the "sprouts" mentioned on Day Three. These were, perhaps, samples of the best of "the herb that yields seed, and the fruit tree that yields fruit" (Genesis 1:11) from Day Three. But these were grown (sprouted) at the command of the Creator right in front of Adam. There could be no mistake. The LORD God was the Owner. Adam was the one created and given delegated authority and responsibility. These trees were provided by the Owner. Adam was given permission to eat of them "freely," but he did not own them.

The two special trees, the Tree of Life and the Tree of the Knowledge of Good and Evil, were unique and were present in the Garden before Adam arrived. Adam was specifically instructed not to eat the fruit of the Tree of the Knowledge of Good and Evil. Punishment was to be swift and sure. Everything else was Adam's to enjoy.

The lesson was clear. The Creator, *Elohim*, the LORD God, was the boss. Adam was given the high privilege of "manager," but ownership rested with the Creator. Failure to acknowledge that most basic of relationships resulted in what we now experience: "the whole creation groans and labors with birth pangs together until now" (Romans 8:22).

The lesson of human distinction

Perhaps the most harmful error of the teachings of naturalistic evolution is that humanity is nothing more than a "higher order" animal. Mankind is taught to be "no better" than their "brothers" in the animal "kingdom."

The People for the Ethical Treatment of Animals (PETA) have espoused a number of "animal rights" (as equal to the various amendments to the Constitution)—and have even suggested that the planet would be better off if much of humanity was eliminated.

It is common for various documentaries to personify animal stories with human-like personalities and thoughts when there is absolutely no evidence of such behavior or ability to "understand" the thoughts of the creatures under study. The only justification for such an imaginary tale is the evolutionary dogma that "we" have descended from the "lower" forms of life and humanity's "developed" characteristics are "reflected" in the lifestyles of animals.

God intended that Adam (and we who are his descendants) would not think that way.

> Out of the ground the LORD God formed every beast of the field and every bird of the air, and brought them to Adam to see what he would call them. And whatever Adam called each living creature, that was its name. So Adam gave names to all cattle, to the birds of the air, and

to every beast of the field. But for Adam there was not found a helper comparable to him. (Genesis 2:19-20)

Adam's book tells the true story. With Adam present, God "formed" representative creatures of the land and the air. This was again a performance by the Creator in front of Adam. The reason for this special repetition of Days Five and Six creation events is clearly stated by God. "And the LORD God said, 'It is not good that man should be alone; I will make him a helper comparable to him'" (Genesis 2:18). Adam needed to see that nothing on earth was "comparable" to him—that he was different than everything else. Adam was created with the "image" of the Creator. All other life did not share that.

When God put Adam to sleep and constructed (formed) the "helper comparable to him," Adam's response was: "This is now bone of my bones and flesh of my flesh; She shall be called Woman, because she was taken out of Man" (Genesis 2:23). Nothing that Adam had seen and named before was anything like God's image. Man was unique. That lesson had to be learned.

Part of genuine benevolent management is humble recognition that God's gift of delegated authority and responsibility involves an assurance of the distinction between the ruler and the ruled. If authority is nothing more than "might" or "chance," then authority means little—and responsibility drops to nothing more than personal gain and greed. Much of what ails world politics in our era is an extension of the rejection of these first two lessons. Thus, man has usurped the ownership of creation and has failed to recognize the unique attributes of his Creator. Man now condones the behavior of the animal he believes himself to be.

The lesson of work

Our Western culture has benefited enormously from the so-called "Protestant Ethic" holding that work is a good thing. Sadly, that ethic is slipping beneath a rising tide of expectation that the benefits of effective work should be distributed without regard to effort or industry. Work has become a disagreeable annoyance rather than a privilege to enjoy.

That was not the lesson God taught Adam in the Garden.

Prior to Adam there was "no man to *till* the ground" (Genesis 2:5). That in itself is instructive. Cattle, creeping things, and beasts of the earth do not "till" the "ground" (land). Whatever God had in mind for man, no other creature could perform it. The living creatures were provided "food" by the hand of their Creator. Many would have instilled in them the ability to survive as God had designed them. Some would come to expect their care from the one God had instructed to "have dominion" over them. All creatures, except man alone, would have no ability or knowledge to "till" the land.

The word choices here are important. The Hebrew term for "till" is *'abad*, and has the basic meaning "to serve." Added to this idea is the instruction to "keep" the Garden. "Then the LORD God took the man and put him in the garden of Eden to *tend* and *keep* it" (Genesis 2:15). The Hebrew term for "keep" is *shamar*, whose basic use is to "guard" or to "observe." Both of these words are used prolifically throughout the Old Testament and always carry the idea of paying attention to the task at hand—either for the benefits of such service or to benefit the one served.

Herein lies the basic "job description" of a manager. With very few guidelines other than to benefit the Owner, a manager has the authority to "rule" and "have dominion," but at the same time is to serve and protect the interests of the Owner.

Jesus provided two clear "parables" to illustrate this responsibility.

Matthew 25:14-30 emphasizes faithfulness—to the Owner. The Owner "travels" to a "far country" and delivers" his (the owner's) "goods" to his servants. He then gives to each "according to his own ability" and leaves them to their own initiative. After a "long time" the Lord returned and "settled" with each one. All of them had doubled what had been given to them—except one. Those with industry and faithfulness were praised as "good and faithful" and were given authority over "many things." The servant who did nothing with what he had been given was called "wicked and lazy" and was thrown out of the presence of the Owner because he was "unprofitable."

The parable in Luke 19:13-27 emphasizes profitableness—for the Owner's sake. A very similar situation is drawn in which a nobleman goes into a "far country" to receive a kingdom. Ten servants are each given a common "pound" with which to trade and increase the nobleman's wealth. When the nobleman returns as King, he asks his servants for a report of their work, "that he might know how much every man had gained by trading." One came and produced ten pounds—a ten-fold return. Another came and produced five pounds—a five-fold return. The profitable servants received reward commensurate with their work. They were given public commendation as good servants and given authority over "cities" proportional to their profitability.

Then came the one with the original pound and no profit. This represented both a loss of opportunity as well as a loss of potential interest merely by passive investment in a "profit making" bank. In both parables the "wicked" servant received nothing but condemnation and loss and was stripped of any reward or honor. What was his in the beginning was taken away and given to the most faithful or most profitable servant.

There is nothing in the Bible that commends non-productive work. There is nothing in the Bible that validates the redistribution of wealth. Yes, pity and mercy to those who are disadvantaged and poor are expected, but there is never the suggestion that work is to be avoided.

To the contrary, God designates man as the responsible party to "serve" and "guard" the land. And that responsibility demands everything that provides the knowledge to do so. There must be the "research and development" necessary to find out how the "land" works. Then once such research has discovered the elements of the land, technology must be developed to use the knowledge gained in effective applications. Man must not only know "what" but "how" as well.

Processes of distribution must be developed to assure obedience to the "fruitful and multiply" side of the equation, and then there must be systems to ensure that the knowledge and technology is passed on to others as future generations enter into life. Serving and guarding the land was part of man's "rule" and "dominion." Work was not designed as an onerous task, but as a specialized privilege of the one who was granted the unique abilities to profit from his work. Essentially such open authority implies the following (in our modern jargon):

- Science uncovers "how" things work and is obedience to the "subdue" mandate.

- Technology uses knowledge to "make" things useful and is obedience to the "rule" mandate.

- Commerce distributes the "useful things" to all and is obedience to the "fill the earth" mandate.

- Education teaches the "specialties" to everyone and is obedience to the "teach all things" mandate.

- Humanities glorifies the Creator with praise and beauty, and obeys the "to the glory of God" mandate.

After Adam and Eve rebelled from their delegated responsibility—so that they could be "free" from the need to "serve" and "guard" the land—their work became a "sorrow" and required "sweat" to eat. That was not God's design. Work was part of the "good" that the Creator had made. Man's rebellion changed all of that.

The lesson to avoid evil

All of Scripture shifts in Genesis 3. This will be discussed in more depth in the next chapter. Here the lesson is simple. Just as there was a Tree of Life, so there was a Tree of the Knowledge of Good and Evil. Adam was free to eat and benefit from the Tree of Life, but was forbidden, upon the pain of death, to eat from the tree that contained the "Knowledge of Good and Evil."

Adam knew good. He was in the magnificent Garden that God

Himself had made. He was given the great freedom to manage the planet under God's ownership as His *steward*. God allowed Adam to know and to name all of the animal creatures with which he would share earth. The freedom to "till" the ground and enjoy the produce of his labor was essentially unlimited. God gave Adam a compatible "helper" who would be his life partner, and the stunning knowledge that the children who would come from their union would "rule" earth. Everything that he could want or imagine to do was in front of him—except evil.

The one prohibition, the only restriction that God had placed on mankind, was the requirement to refrain from the knowledge of evil.

Obviously, that restriction and the accompanying warning were insufficient to keep Adam and Eve from believing that they could disobey the Creator—and get away with it. In that, they were much like Lucifer who rebelled in heaven. He thought himself to be smart enough, powerful enough, with enough influence to usurp the One who had created him.

> "I will ascend into heaven, I will exalt my throne above the stars of God; I will also sit on the mount of the congregation On the farthest sides of the north; I will ascend above the heights of the clouds, I will be like the Most High." (Isaiah 14:13-14)

Thus Eve "listened" to the clever argument of the serpent, allowed herself to be deceived, and openly disobeyed that one restriction. Adam, whom the Scripture clearly tells us was not deceived (1 Timothy 2:14), consciously, willingly, knowingly rebelled—in spite of his personal instruction in the Garden and all the evidence to the contrary. Adam chose to know "evil."

The promise of the Creator

God in His sovereignty surely knew that creating a being with such enormous capacity for liberty and close fellowship would allow for the possibility of rebellion. God wills love. Love requires choice.

Choice allows evil. Yet that knowledge in no way negated the provision for a perfect relationship with the Creator. And even though the Creator surely understood that an "evil" choice would be made, back in the councils of eternity the Triune Godhead made provision for redemption, "not willing that any should perish" (2 Peter 3:9).

The lessons were given. These two students rejected the information.

That, however, did not negate the "speech" and "knowledge" of the great creation and the personal lessons of the great Creator. Those who "receive" the Creator today are given "the right to become children of God" (John 1:12).

CHAPTER EIGHT
THE BEGINNING OF SIN AND DEATH

Everything changed in the Garden of Eden.

All that we observe, all that we know, all that we feel today is viewed through the lens of sin and death. All of theology must deal with the concept of sin. All of science must deal with the reality of death. Nothing in our world can be properly evaluated without some consideration of what sin is and how death impacts reality.

The evolutionary naturalist refuses to set any sort of definition on "sin" and insists that "death" is a natural process that ultimately generates the "better" product. The biblical text insists that sin is the product of willful rebellion against the Creator and that death is the judgment against that rebellion. Evolution demands eons of chaos, death, and destruction as necessary tools of "natural selection" to weed out the environmentally unfit. The Bible contends that the original environment was pristine and the "most fit" of God's creation quickly disdained that perfection and suffered a horrible punishment. Very different messages.

But before it is possible to approach these issues, it is absolutely necessary to grasp what has been revealed about the origin of the universe. One may reject that information, but all logic demands a reason for the rejection—or an admission that one's presupposition eliminates the data revealed.

God's Summary Evaluation

> Then God saw everything that He had made, and indeed it was very good. So the evening and the morning were the sixth day. Thus the heavens and the earth, and all the host of them, were finished. And on the seventh day God ended His work which He had done, and He rested on the seventh day from all His work which He had done. Then God blessed the seventh day and sanctified it, because in it He rested from all His work which God had created and made. (Genesis 1:31 through 2:1-3)

Everything was very good

The repetition of God's comment is worth noting. Five of the six working days of the creation week are pronounced "good" by the Creator. It is the same Hebrew word each time, and means just what is expected: good, pleasant, agreeable, excellent, of benefit, etc. There is nothing very unusual about the word, except that it is repeated so often and that it is God who uses the term.

Whatever is in view by the text, the One who pronounces the evaluation must shape the meaning of the term. That is, if you or I used the term, our meaning would be colored by our own experience, education, opinions, intellect, persuasions, etc. My "good" and your "good" could well imply different things. Some societies would approve of certain kinds of murder as a "good" thing. Most, however, would not. As noted above, the evolutionary naturalist believes death to be a "good" process. The Bible does not.

Given that the Creator is the One using the term, a careful application of the text would have to consider the character of the Evaluator—gaining understanding of His attributes—before rendering an opinion of the meaning of the term "good" as it applies to the creation itself.

God is holy

This the preeminent attribute of the Creator God. Whatever God does or says, He must reveal truth. Scripture insists that the God of creation is the same God of salvation. The love that drives Him to become man and die a substitutionary death for our sins is driven by the holiness that demands justice for the horrible rebellion against that very holiness.

> 1 Samuel 2:2 – No one is holy like the Lord, For there is none besides You, Nor is there any rock like our God.

> Exodus 15:11 – Who is like You, O Lord, among the gods? Who is like You, glorious in holiness, Fearful in praises, doing wonders?

> Deuteronomy 32:3-4 – I proclaim the name of the Lord…For all His ways are justice, A God of truth and without injustice; Righteous and upright is He.

> Romans 3:26 – …that He might be just and the justifier of the one who has faith in Jesus.

God must reveal truth—He cannot lie (Titus 1:2). God must reveal truth in the created "things" of the universe. The creation could not "distort" anything about God—or about the creation itself. God could not make anything that would inexorably lead us to a wrong conclusion. God could not create processes that would counter His own nature, or that would lead us to conclude something untrue about Him. Whatever God did or said would have to be "true and righteous altogether" (Psalm 19:9).

God is omniscient

This is God's most easily observable attribute. Design and order and function are everywhere known and observed. Everywhere we can look—up into the deepest recesses of space or down into the minutia of the microscope—the intricacy, precision, and complexity of all things stagger us with detail, information, and order. The First Cause of all of our reality must have all knowledge as well as all power.

Psalm 104:24 – O LORD, how manifold are Your works! In wisdom You have made them all.

Isaiah 46:9-10 – I am God, and there is none like Me,

Acts 15:18 – Known to God from eternity are all His works.

1 Corinthians 14:33 – For God is not the author of confusion but of peace, as in all the churches of the saints.

Hebrews 6:16-18 – Thus God…confirmed it by an oath, that by two immutable things, in which it is impossible for God to lie, we might have strong consolation, who have fled for refuge to lay hold of the hope set before us.

The consistent message of Scripture is that God is not unaware of anything. God cannot be progressively aware. God's knowledge is immediate. God is free from imperfection. God knows all there is to know. God's purpose and order flow from His omniscience. His decisions are unchangeable and without confusion. God's specific will and pleasure are always implemented. These statements are not ambiguous. They are either true as presented or they are an awful lie. They must either be believed as presented or rejected out of hand.

God is love

Surely this side to the nature of God is so commonly known it cannot be refuted—except by those who have embraced the idea that God does not exist. Those who are the twice-born of God are intimately aware of the drawing of the Holy Spirit. "We love Him because He first loved us" (1 John 4:19).

What may not always be easily understood is that because God is love, God could not exploit the senseless death of millions of life forms just to arrive where He wanted to be all along. Nor could God use the wasteful and cruel processes of naturalistic evolution to "create" a universe that would "speak" the "invisible" nature of His "Godhead" (Romans 1:20; Psalm 19:1-3).

God's flawless "good"

Whatever God said was "good" would have to be in harmony with His divine nature. Since God is holy, He cannot deceive us about the order of the creation week. Since God is omniscient, He would not guess or use "trial and error" methodology. God must reveal complete information, or else keep information secret (Deuteronomy 29:29).

God would not experiment. Since He knows, He must do. God would not produce "inferior" things. He can do only "holy" acts. He cannot create, make, or shape non-functional processes. The belief of atheistic evolution requires both experimentation with creation and the creation of inferior forms. In evolution, there is no permanent "good." Evolutionary naturalism requires the use of processes and the sanction of that which is the opposite of God's nature.

All of this clear evidence and observation requires that we who read the text of Genesis 1 understand "good" to mean "flawless perfection."

God's "good" is flawless function

God could not deceive us into thinking that the universe was immensely old. God's own account of His work specifies His organization and purpose for the things that were made. The universe must function flawlessly from the beginning.

Because God is omniscient, everything in that universe must work as designed. Because God is omnipotent, absolutely everything would have absolutely everything it needed to operate, live, reproduce, and populate under the orders and in agreement with the Creator's design. Each and every component was designed to function without flaw. Every part had to work as ordered, and all living things must have functioned under the limits and in the places for their life. Nothing was left to chance. Nothing was misplaced or out of place.

God's "good" could not include sin

Since God is holy, there could be no "sin." Sin, of course, is that which is contrary and/or in rebellion against the holiness of God. For the holy, omniscient, omnipotent, loving Creator to conclude that everything He had created and made was "very good," there could be nothing in that completed creation that was not functioning flawlessly or was in conscious rebellion against the immutable nature of the Creator.

Sin, as will be explored later in this chapter, was introduced into the creation by Adam.

God's "good" could not include death

God is life. Everything that is revealed about God centers on His eternal Being. The most personal names that God reveals is the *Yaweh*—the "I am"—the One who exists by the right and nature of who He is. Jesus insists the He is "the way, the truth, and the life" (John 14:6). The awesome *Apokalypsis* of Jesus Christ opens with the "loud voice, as of a trumpet, saying, 'I am the Alpha and the Omega, the First and the Last'" (Revelation 1:10-11). There can be no mistake. God *is* life.

There is absolutely no indication anywhere in the Scriptures that the living God created death. Nothing in the Bible suggests that death was a part of the "good" creation that God made in His work-week of six days.

Death in Scripture is separation from God. Death stops life. Death intrudes into and destroys everything. Death is _not_ normal. Death is the result of sin and death is the "last enemy" that will be destroyed by the longsuffering Redeemer Himself (1 Corinthians 15:26).

Because of who God is, we can be assured of a creation that functioned as designed—a creation cosmology that "fits" the Creator. When God completed His work, *He* pronounced "everything that He had made, and indeed it was very good" (Genesis 1:31). If words are going to mean anything at all, "good" must include the flawless functioning of every molecule and all systems and all life as the omniscient Creator would design. It would also demand that there was nothing out of order or in rebellion to His nature—that means there was no sin or death in all of the creation—until Genesis 3.

The seventh day

> And on the seventh day God ended His work which He had done, and He rested on the seventh day from all His work which He had done. Then God blessed the seventh day and sanctified it, because in it He rested from all His work which God had created and made. (Genesis 2:2-3)

It is clear from several other passages in the Bible that God intended us to understand that the pattern set by the Creator was to be followed by all who would later walk the earth. Centuries later when Moses met with God on the mountain in Sinai to receive the Ten Commandments, God specifically insisted that the new nation of Israel was to "remember" this rest day as a "holy" day: "For in six days the LORD made the heavens and the earth, the sea, and all that is in them, and rested the seventh day. Therefore the LORD blessed the Sabbath day and hallowed it" (Exodus 20:11).

Much later Jesus Himself would tell the legalistic Pharisees that "the Sabbath was made for man, and not man for the Sabbath" (Mark 2:27). God *designed* the work week after the manner of the creation week. The Pharisees had made a mockery of what God intended for all humanity to follow. The Hebrew *Shabbath* means "cease" or "rest" (not Saturday). Even though the end of the work week was "Saturday" for Israel, the formal "Sabbaths" occurred on many different days of the month and week (e.g., Leviticus 23:24-39).

Western society has changed this emphasis a bit because "Christianity" celebrates the resurrection on the "first day of the week" (Mark 16:9). Many nations extend the "rest" period to more than one day, but the original pattern was to work six days and rest one. In fact, the seven-day week is a unique pattern. All astronomical "clocks" are not divisible by seven. The lunar month is 29.53059 days. The solar year is 365.24219 days. Neither of which is divisible by seven. Furthermore, the movement of the solar system within the galaxy and the movements of the galaxy within the universe, as far as we are able to clock them, are not divisible by seven either.

Evidently, God designed the "rest day" for humanity, just like He said.

Rebellion in the Heavens

The angelic host appears to have been created on the first or second day of creation. It seems clear that the "sons of God" were functioning and watching God's marvelous creative actions at least by the third day when the "foundations of the earth" were laid (Job 38:4-7). It is also clear from Scripture that the angelic host was designed as independent spirit beings (Psalm 104:5) to "minister" to those who would become the "heirs of salvation" (Hebrews 1:14). They have some ranking system of power and authority recognized by the terms "principalities and powers" frequently mentioned in the New Testament.

There are multiplied billions of them. A short cameo is given in the book of Revelation where the assembly surrounding the Throne of God includes "ten thousand times ten thousand, and thousands of thousands" of heavenly beings (Revelation 5:11), and the angelic creatures compose an "innumerable company" (Hebrews 12:22). They can also assume human form for special purposes (Genesis 19:1, 5; Matthew 16:5; Acts 1:10; Hebrews 13:2; etc.). They are far more powerful than humans (Psalm 103:20), yet are very interested in the unique work of God among humanity (Ephesians 3:10; 1 Peter 1:12).

Three of the angelic leaders are named in Scripture. Lucifer is an "Arch" angel who appears to be connected to the ministry of God the Father (Ezekiel 28:13-17). Gabriel seems to be connected to the ministry of the Holy Spirit (Daniel 8:16; 9:21; Zacharias in Luke 1:19 and Mary in Luke 1:26), and Michael seems to be connected to the ministry of the Son of God (Daniel 10:13, 21; 12:1; Jude 1:9; Revelation 12:7).

Lucifer figures into the study of sin and death because it is commonly understood that he was instrumental in the deception of Eve. Here's a quick review of biblical data relating to Lucifer and his place in the world.

Lucifer is recognized throughout Scripture by three main titles.

- The Dragon (Revelation 20:2; 12:3-9; Isaiah 27:1)
- The Devil (Matthew 4:1-11; John 8:44; Ephesians 6:11; 1 Peter 5:8)
- The Adversary, often transliterated as "Satan" (Job 1 and 2; Zechariah 3:1-2; Luke 22:3, 31; Revelation 20:7)

Lucifer is described in two major passages in the Old Testament.

- Isaiah 14:12-15, which tells of his change of heart, his purpose in rebelling, and his defeat and his ultimate imprisonment in Sheol.
- Ezekiel 28:12-17, which identifies him as the "anointed cherub who covers," whose wisdom and beauty led him to believe that he could overthrow the God of creation.

Lucifer was displaced from his heavenly position and becomes the Adversary.

- A war in heaven occurred in which one third of the angelic host followed in rebellion (Revelation 12:2-9). It is not precisely clear that this event took place during early history, but it appears to describe what had taken place in the past.
- Jesus himself speaks of Lucifer falling from heaven as though it was a past event (Luke 10:18).

All of these passages lend support to the awareness of Lucifer's direct involvement with the event described in Genesis 3. The Lord Jesus later specifically lays the blame for the death of Adam and Eve at the feet of Lucifer when He says: "He [the Devil] was a murderer from the beginning, and does not stand in the truth, because there is no truth in him. When he speaks a lie, he speaks from his own resources, for he is a liar and the father of it" (John 8:44).

> So the great dragon was cast out, that serpent of old, called the Devil and Satan, who deceives the whole world; he was cast to the earth, and his angels were cast out with him. (Revelation 12:9)

Rebellion in the Garden

Many have wondered how much time elapsed between the end of Day Seven and the world-changing events at the Tree of the Knowledge of Good and Evil. No specific time period is stated, but it does not appear that it would not have been very long. Eve did not "conceive" until after this event, after the pronouncement of the judgments, and after they had been cast out of the Garden (Genesis 4:1). Given the basic command to "be fruitful and multiply," it is unlikely that Adam and Eve would have delayed their attempt to fulfill this mandate.

However one interprets the information, it could not have been "ages." More than likely it would have been less than a year, and probably only a few days after they both had been created.

Enter the serpent

Genesis 3 opens with the "serpent" already in the Garden and in the process of speaking with Eve. Just what this creature was at the time of its creation is not known. The Hebrew word, *nachash*, is only used 30 other times in the Old Testament and each instance refers to the "snake" of modern taxonomy. An almost identical term is translated "enchanter" or "diviner."

Since the subsequent information in Genesis 3 indicates that the original shape and function of this creature was vastly changed by God for its participation in the horrible rebellion of humanity, we have little idea of the original nature of this "beast of the field." Whatever may have been its appearance, it is clear from Scripture that the modern "snake" has little to offer our understanding of that unique event.

Ezekiel tells us that Lucifer had been "in the garden of God" (Ezekiel 28:13) and was a dazzling creature of stunning beauty and immense wisdom. Adam tells us in his record that the serpent "was more cunning than any beast of the field" (Genesis 3:1). It is known from many instances in Scripture that angelic powers include the ability to "possess" the bodies of man and animals (Matthew 8:12; Mark 5:12; etc.). It is certainly plausible, therefore, to think that the most ambitious, powerful, and intelligent Archangel would seek to possess the most "clever" of the beasts of the field through which to accomplish his plan.

Neither Eve nor Adam show surprise at the conversational ability of the serpent. Remember, at least Adam had seen each kind of the animals when God brought them to him for naming. Surely, if this "serpent" suddenly began to debate with Eve, the reaction would have been much different. As recorded, Adam (who was "with her") remained passive and silent. Lucifer rarely acts in spectacular ways. "And no wonder! for Satan himself transforms himself into an angel of light. Therefore it is no great thing if his ministers also transform themselves into ministers of righteousness" (2 Corinthians 11:14-15).

Satan's strategy

In these first few verses of Genesis 3, a profound insight is revealed of how the Adversary will approach humanity for the rest of time. One can search the Scriptures and find many examples of just this same strategy throughout both the Old and New Testaments. Tactics have and will change over time and culture, but the strategy remains the same.

Perhaps it is worthwhile to review the status as chapter 3 begins. God had previously set only one "prohibition" for Adam and Eve. They were given free access to all the "trees" of the Garden. The special "estate" of the Creator was abounding with everything good, but they were commanded not to eat from the Tree of the Knowledge of Good and Evil. They had free access to all "good" things and certainly had knowledge of the Creator's "good." They were *only* prohibited from knowing "evil." God had given clear and precise warning against any disobedience to His one restriction.

> And the Lord God commanded the man, saying, "Of every tree of the garden you may freely eat; but of the tree of the knowledge of good and evil you shall not eat, for in the day that you eat of it you shall surely die. (Genesis 2:16-17)

All is "good." Adam and Eve have enjoyed fellowship with the Creator and the lush beauty and plenty of the garden "east of Eden" that God Himself had made for their pleasure. Instructions are clear. Complete provisions are made, and all eternity is before them. It is at this point in time that Satan initiates the "lie" and the "murder" in the revelation of his worldwide and age-long strategy to deceive (John 8:44).

Doubt the Word

Genesis 3:1 opens with the serpent asking Eve the question: "Has God indeed said, 'You shall not eat of every tree of the garden'?" Quite clever, actually. The question did not appear to be a threat. No doubt the fresh and lush beauty of the Tree of the Knowledge of Good and Evil did not appear to be "not good." Every opportunity was there at that moment for Eve to pull away from any implied suggestion that God had not said what He had clearly stated—but the age-long battle had begun.

Satan introduced the element of doubt into the world.

It is at this place and in this manner that every human since the Garden event has been initially tempted. Before minds are consciously corrupted, before events have seared hearts and burdened lives with sin, and before time has elapsed beyond the moments where decisions can be made, Satan confronts with: "Has God indeed said?"

This doubt is presented in a wide variety of questions today. How can we know that the Bible is the "real" Word of God? Is the version or the translation of the Bible that is available to us the same one that

God caused to be recorded? Hasn't scholarship proven that the Bible is incorrect in many places? Aren't there errors in the Bible? How can we trust what we read? Everybody seems to have a different opinion of what the Bible words mean—how do we know which opinion is correct?

There are numerous ways to cast doubt. It's easy to do. Far more people seem to doubt the authority and accuracy of the Bible than agree to it. Nobody's perfect, therefore nothing is perfect. Nothing turns out as it was expected. All experience verifies that absolutes do not exist. Why should one expect anything different from the Bible?

Doubt about God's Word opens the door to the "knowledge" of "evil."

Deny the Word

Once Eve had responded with a partially correct repetition of what God had told them about the restricted tree and the consequences of disobedience, Satan responded with: "You will not surely die" (Genesis 3:4). This, of course, is a direct denial of the ability of the Creator to do what He had said He would do. Once doubt has been entertained and the possibility of error or ignorance on the part of God is accepted, the likelihood of inability or hesitation on the part of God seems reasonable.

After all, many people make threats that they do not intend to do or cannot carry out. It would seem perfectly possible for such to be the case with God. Doesn't the Bible talk about God "repenting" from a previous decision? Aren't there instances in the Bible where God either changes His mind or delays His judgment? Surely this is nothing more than logical reasoning. God may have threated to kill Adam and Eve if they "ate" of that tree, but it is not likely that the God of love would ever punish His creation so severely.

However, this is much more than mere speculation on the part of Satan. He insists that they will "surely" not die. No beating around the bush in this defiant statement. God either will not or cannot do as He said. There is no ambiguity. Either Satan is right and God is wrong, or God is right and Satan is wrong. There can be no harmony of these two possibilities.

Denial of God's Word demands the choice between good and "evil."

Denigrate the Word

Once doubt and denial have been accepted, it is but a short step to conclude that God Himself has a flawed character. Lucifer has now completed the gulf that will forever separate the creature from the Creator. Although Eve was deceived (1 Timothy 2:14), Adam was not.

> Then the serpent said to the woman, "You will not surely die. For God knows that in the day you eat of it your eyes will be opened, and you will be like God, knowing good and evil. (Genesis 3:4-5)

There is a twofold denigration in this statement. First, God has lied. He is not holy. He is trying to intimidate. His goodness is all a sham. God has lied.

Second, God is withholding "good" from you. God is selfish. God is not omnipotent. He knows that eating of this forbidden fruit will empower you with the same "knowledge" that God has. If you listen to God, you will remain weak and impotent. Eat and you will be "like God."

Denigrating God closes the door of evil behind us and gives Satan the win.

Eve's deception

God had said:

> "Of every tree of the garden you may freely eat; but of the tree of the knowledge of good and evil you shall not eat, for in the day that you eat of it you shall surely die." (Genesis 2:16-17)

Eve responded to Satan:

> "We may eat the fruit of the trees of the garden; but of the fruit of the tree which is in the midst of the garden, God has said, 'You shall not eat it, nor shall you touch it, lest you die.'" (Genesis 3:2-3)

Eve's response reveals the pattern for all sinful humanity. She misapplied or misunderstood God's Word. Eve subtracted the generosity of God by ignoring the liberty to "freely eat" of "every" tree in the garden except the Tree of the Knowledge of Good and Evil. Eve also added an unusual interpretation about the restriction by suggesting that God prohibited them from even "touching" the fruit.

She failed to rebuke or question the serpent. She failed to seek counsel or assert obedience. She should have rejected this lie. Having entertained doubt about the precise words of God, Eve remains silent when Lucifer flatly pronounces that God would not do as He said. Then when Satan insists that God is selfish and is withholding some exquisite privilege from them, Eve "bites" the lie and "eats" the fruit.

Eve's decision illustrates the classic pattern of those who are lured into temptation.

Evil is attractive physically

Eve notes that the fruit was "good for food." She had access to all the other fruits. She did not actually *need* the fruit. It does not appear that she was even hungry. How many have fallen into sin merely because the "lusts of the flesh" have taken them away from the security and safety of God's grace? Western society is drifting more and more into the deception of sinful behavior, but all societies ache when "evil" strikes with murder or adultery. Crimes of passion ripple throughout the world.

Satan did his job well.

Evil is attractive aesthetically

Once Eve had desired the "taste" of evil, she began to notice that the fruit of the forbidden tree was "pleasant to the eyes." She lived in the most beautiful estate ever made. She enjoyed total perfection! What possible beauty could rival the matchless "good" of the omnipotent and omniscient Creator?

Yes, but *this* beauty is here now. Yesterday's breathtaking delight is a faded memory. Here, now, is the sparkling and mesmerizing "lust of the eyes" that rings out the mellow song of pleasurable fulfillment. Here, now, is the exquisite dazzle of the unexperienced enchantment. Such beauty could not contain evil. It must be a good thing.

Many have fallen since that fateful day to the siren's call of the aesthetically beautiful. The Greek legend may well reflect the seduction of Eve as she listened to the serpent and gazed longingly on the forbidden fruit. "Flee" from the stirring passions, the Scripture warn. "Follow" after righteousness with the godly. "Fear" the Lord is the oft-repeated command.

Eve did none of those.

Evil is attractive mentally

And finally, the *coup de grace*—this action is "desired to make wise." This delicious and delectable fruit that a selfish God had forbidden, held the secret to true wisdom! Now, with just a simple action, ultimate power and knowledge was to be had. What a sad commentary on the mind of man. Eve *had* knowledge of "good." She already enjoyed daily fellowship with the One who had created her. Whatever might have been lacking in her practical wisdom could readily be learned and applied through the liberty that had been granted. What more could she possibly want?

"To be like God, knowing good and evil."

This tree—this *forbidden* tree—was the secret to all knowledge. All she had to do was "eat" and everything would be hers. The serpent was so beautiful and so clever. God was aloof and only around when it suited Him. The opportunity was enormous. The timing was perfect. God was not around to stop her.

So "…she took of its fruit and ate" (Genesis 3:6).

Adam's rebellion

The Bible is very clear on this point. Eve had been fooled into the sin that brought about her death, but Adam was not tempted by the argument from the serpent. He heard every word. He was "with her," his own record states (Genesis 3:6). Adam was the one who consciously, willingly, knowingly chose to reject the word of his Creator and embrace the rebellion of Lucifer.

> Adam was first formed, then Eve. And Adam was not deceived. (1 Timothy 2:13-14)
>
> Therefore, just as through one man sin entered the world, and death through sin, and thus death spread to all men. (Romans 5:12)
>
> For as in Adam all die, even so in Christ shall all be made alive. (1 Corinthians 15:22)

There can be no doubt of the message from the Scripture. Eve led the way through her gullibility. She listened to the serpent. She clearly disobeyed God's command. Adam, however, openly rebelled.

Whatever may have been his private thoughts during the debate between the serpent and Eve, he knew what he was doing when he accepted the offer of the fruit from Eve. Perhaps he may have reasoned that God could make him another "Eve" if she died when she ate the fruit. Perhaps he only desired the ultimate freedom from restrictions. Perhaps Adam thought that he could join in Lucifer's rebellion and be rewarded for his duplicity. Adam's motivation is not revealed. But his actions surely are, and the result of that awful moment still rings throughout the universe.

Adam sinned.

Judgment in the Garden

Not much commentary needs to be added to the words of Scripture. The judgment of God that follows Eve's deception and Adam's rebellion sets the conditions for earth's inhabitants and environmental structure for millennia to come.

Satan appears to have some freedom yet (Job 1, 2), but his judgment is sure (Revelation 20). Much of our spiritual life confronts the spiritual warfare "against principalities, against powers, against the rulers of the darkness of this age, against spiritual hosts of wickedness in the heavenly places" (Ephesians 6:12), but our earthly struggles and our physical struggles stem directly from the judgment of God on those who had participated in rebellion.

The serpent becomes the age-long enemy of man

- It is cursed above all other animals.

- It is to crawl on it belly and "eat" dust.

- It is to have constant enmity against mankind.

- It is to injure the seed of the woman, but will receive mortal injury from the woman's seed (3:15).

Many Bible scholars refer to this as the "first gospel," interpreting the "seed of the woman" to be Christ. This concept is certainly borne out in the message of the gospel, but this curse may also refer to the age-long physical battle between mankind and serpents.

The woman (all women) are forever altered

- The "shame" of nakedness now dominates (Genesis 3:7; Exodus 32:25; Revelation 3:18).

- The woman will have "greatly multiplied sorrow."
    - (Hebrew: *itstabown* "worrisomeness")
    - An increase in her childbearing "toil"

- The woman will also "long" for her husband.
    - (Hebrew: *etseb*) = "ache," "desire"

184

- Her husband would "have power" (Hebrew: *mashal*) over her

The man (as head of all humanity) bears total responsibility

- Man's relationship to the earth is forever altered.

- The "ground" (literally, "earth" or "elements") became cursed because of Adam's sin (Romans 8:20-22; Hebrews 1:10-12; 1 Peter 1:24).

This "curse" on the "ground" is still felt today. Paul makes the comment to his Roman readers that "the whole creation groans and labors with birth pangs together until now" (Romans 8:22). Science recognizes this phenomenon as a universal law: the Second Law of Thermodynamics.

Much has been written on this subject, but all have learned in early schooling that matter cannot be created or destroyed and that when that matter-energy is used, some of the energy becomes unusable. "Work" always takes its toll. One can take energy from one source and temporarily increase the capacity to "work" in another, but ultimately everything "dies."

The serpent and Eve each received a personal judgment fitting their involvement. Adam, however, both as the federal head of the human race and because of his open and conscious rebellion, caused a judgment to fall on the "ground" of creation.

The curse on man was fourfold:

- Sorrow – Resulting from continual disappointment and futility.

- Pain and Suffering – Signified by the "thorns" which hinder man in his efforts to provide a living.

- Sweat and Tears – From intense struggle against a hostile environment.

- Physical Death would eventually triumph over all man's efforts.

The redemption process is also revealed

Sin and death now dominate creation. Man has become separated from the life of God and is born with a nature that will inevitably rebel against the Creator. Such a setting would be utter futility were it not for the prescient foreknowledge of the Creator displayed in the effort to redeem Adam and Eve from their doom.

In the immediate actions of our Creator for Adam and Eve, you and I are encouraged to trust His later provision in time with "the Lamb slain from the foundation of the world" (Revelation 13:8). Over four thousand years beyond the day of judgment on earth would come the Redeemer with the price necessary to buy all humanity back from death. Genesis 3 illustrates what God would do in the future, as well as what He did do for the immediate need.

God made coats of skins and clothed them. An animal was killed to provide the covering. This "covering" of their nakedness foreshadowed the "day of atonement" that would later be instituted as a formal sacrifice to "cover" the sins of the nation of Israel. God had rested from creating and would not have "created" skins, but would have "made" them. Adam and Eve would have witnessed the killing. The example of the "innocent sacrifice" would have been clearly instilled in Adam and Eve's mind.

God then cast them out of the Garden of Eden and they were forced away from an "eternal life" in sin and decay. Even in His severe judgment, God set a guard against the possibility that Adam and Eve would re-enter the Garden, "lest he put out his hand and take also of the tree of life, and eat, and live forever" (Genesis 3:22).

Death encompasses everything

The death judgment is due to Adam's sin and rebellion.

"...because thou has hearkened unto the voice of thy

wife, and hast eaten of the tree, of which I commanded thee, saying, Thou shalt not eat of it." (Genesis 3:17)

Death is "cessation" of physical life. Death is "separation" from God, who *is* life.

John 5:26 – For as the Father hath life in himself; so hath he given to the Son to save life in himself.

John 14:6 – Jesus saith unto him, "I am the way, the truth, and the life: no man cometh unto the Father, but by me."

The creation "death" is clearly defined in Scripture.

...the creation was subjected to futility, not willingly, but because of Him who subjected it in hope; because the creation itself also will be delivered from the bondage of corruption into the glorious liberty of the children of God. For we know that the whole creation groans and labors with birth pangs together until now. Not only that, but we also who have the firstfruits of the Spirit, even we ourselves groan within ourselves, eagerly waiting for the adoption, the redemption of our body. (Romans 8:20-22)

"You, Lord, in the beginning laid the foundation of the earth, And the heavens are the work of Your hands. They will perish, but You remain; And they will all grow old like a garment; Like a cloak You will fold them up, And they will be changed. But You are the same, And Your years will not fail." Hebrews 1:10-12

The biblical data is widespread throughout the New Testament.

Romans 5:12 – Adam was the "cause" of sin and its consequence.

Romans 5:18; 1 Peter 2:24 – Jesus Christ is the "cure" through His substitutionary death and victorious resurrection.

John 3:3, 5; 1 Peter 1:23 – A "new creation" is necessary to escape death.

2 Peter 3:13 – The Creator will *re*-create a totally perfect universe

If physical death is sanctioned by God through the original creation, that makes God the Author of death. That would make creation "reveal" (according to Romans 1:20) a death-loving God. How could this be? What would salvation be? What would we be "rescued" from? The Bible calls death the "last enemy" and insists that the Lord Jesus will destroy it. If God Himself created "death," then why would He destroy it later? Did God deliberately confuse us?

If death is *not* the judgment for sin as the Bible insists, then the whole of the gospel message is foolishness. If death is not the judgment for sin, then the death of the Lord Jesus on the cross at Calvary is nothing more than a foolish end to an idealist—a martyr killed for a delusion.

The Bible demands that an innocent sacrifice be substituted for the awful sin of humanity. Christ's death is required for salvation. The twice-born are "sanctified" through the offering of the body of Jesus Christ on Calvary (Hebrews 10:10), which was done just once, with and for eternal consequences (Hebrews 10:12-14).

Twisting the words of Scripture so that Christ's physical death had no meaning is a terrible heresy. If there were eons of pain, suffering, and death before the awful rebellion of Adam, then a whole sweep of biblical teaching is thrown into the black hole of allegory.

Humanity must be resurrected

There are different kinds of "flesh" identified by Paul in 1 Corinthians 15:39. Other creatures are "living" things that do not take part in the resurrection. All are specifically separated from the "celestial" creation (1 Corinthians 15:40), like stars and angels.

The "earthy" image of "flesh and blood" cannot inherit the Kingdom of God (1 Corinthians 15:50). God requires a "change" from the physical to the spiritual, from the temporal to the eternal. That change was made possible by the work of Jesus Christ and proven by the resurrection.

Physical changes are required. Resurrection is the absolute opposite of physical death. "Corruption" must become "incorruption." "Dishonor" must become "glory." "Weakness" must become "power." The "natural" must become "spiritual." Physical death is an "intrusion" into the natural order of things and it takes a resurrection to correct it.

The "new man" must be created.

The gospel message insists on the "birth from above" (John 3:3), which brings about a transfer from death to life (John 5:24). It involves a "new creation" (2 Corinthians 5:17). That positional change is a "pledge" of the Holy Spirit (2 Corinthians 5:5).

We await the fulfillment of that promise when our "vile" bodies will be freed from the curse of death (1 Corinthians 15:50; Philippians 3:21; 1 John 3:2; Revelation 21:4-5).

CHAPTER NINE
THE RISE OF CIVILIZATION

The Garden was shut.

God had placed Cheribim with a great sword that turned and whirled like a great scythe at the gate to the Garden. Although the Garden would remain as a testimony to the Creator's greatness, it would also remain forbidden and sealed until the great Flood destroyed the world. Nothing would ever be the same again.

The Process of Time

The early chapters of Genesis are very selective in the presentation of the information that God wanted to reveal. Chapter 1 covers one week—just the six days of creation and the structuring of the universe and the day of rest. Chapter 2 gives the unique perspective of Adam and his experience during Day Six. All of the events in Genesis 2 likely cover several hours and give some of the pertinent details of Adam's awareness and the personal making of the "helper" for Adam, the one who would become the "mother of all living." Genesis 3, the pivotal point in recorded history, covers just a few moments. God has carefully provided a structural outline upon which all Scripture rests.

- God is the Creator

- Man is the delegated steward

- Man is the rebel sinner

- Sin and death reign on earth

- God is the Judge and Redeemer

As the rest of history unfolds, the detail revealed all relates to the foundational messages of Genesis 1-3. One cannot make theological sense or biblical application of what follows without understanding these key elements. It is really impossible to understand God's message without understanding Genesis.

The long lives

Legends abound about races of long-lived people. Various stories about "elves" and other "first-born" creatures are replete throughout literature. One of the more famous is *The Lord of the Rings*, an epic written by J. R. R. Tolkien. Although a fantasy novel with an evolutionary theme, the main characters interact with a race of "Men of Westernese" and "Elves" who represent ancient races that have lived for hundreds of years. Woven throughout are hints of a world disaster by water and evil "lords" and good "wizards" who wage an ongoing semi-spiritual war that has raged for ages.

That and other such epochs are echoes of the historical account in the early chapters of Genesis. Adam is said to have lived 930 years. Methuselah, the oldest human ever recorded, lived 969 years. Several births and deaths of key leaders are recorded (much as one would expect in a genealogical account), with average ages of some 900 years. The obvious question: are these ages "real" years, or are they some sort of figurative language?

Some commentaries suggest that these years are really months, making the average age more like 75—typical of much of human history. The problem immediately surfaces, however, when the ages of various births are noted. Seth, Adam's son, was born when Adam was 130 years old. If the "years" are "months," then Adam was not quite 11 years old when Seth (at least the third child) was born. Seth was 105 when his son Enos was born, making Seth less than nine years old. Enos was only 7.5 years old when his son Cainan was born (if the years were months). Cainan would not yet have been 6 years old (70 divided by 12) when his son, Mahalaleel, was born. Other records present similar problems.

Once again, the record either stands accurate as presented, or is totally absurd.

There does appear to be at least three main reasons why God would have preserved the records of genealogies in these earliest chapters. First, and perhaps most obvious, the record is what one would expect of an actual historical genealogy. The factual, brief data are precisely what would be done by a careful historian documenting previous events. The list in Genesis 5 must be taken at face value—or rejected as if made up entirely of imagination.

Secondarily, the factual accounts give a precise trace, from event to event, that verifies the total span of history. Some have objected to the naming of the various heirs, suggesting that the named children were later grandchildren. It really does not matter. Each record is from a certain date to a second specific event. Genesis 5 contains nine events, beginning with the age of Adam at the birth of Seth to the age of Lamech at the birth of Noah. Genesis 7 provides the tenth event, citing the age of Noah on the very day that the Flood came and destroyed the world.

Thus, by adding the sum of the various event occurrences, it is straightforward event-to-event mathematics; the number of generations between events is irrelevant. Allowing for the potential of an early or late birth event (plus or minus 9 months), the maximum error bar for these ten events would be less than 20 years. The factual record of events in Genesis 5, along with the age given for Noah at the beginning of the Flood, gives the time covered by the first six chapters of Genesis as 1,638 to 1,674 years in duration. Simple addition gives 1,656 years.

There are an additional nine events recorded in Genesis 11 that provide the total time elapsed from creation to the birth of Abraham.

Again, allowing for unknown gestation periods, the 19 total events linking creation to the historically verifiable birth of Abraham (early 2nd millennium B.C.) cover no fewer than 1,948 years and no more than 1,985.

Nothing in the Scripture allows for vast ages. The detailed chronology of the genealogical events demands a recent creation, somewhere on the order of 6,100 years ago!

Finally, these long lives provide excellent insight into the "good" design of the Creator and the inevitable and horrible degeneration of humanity in rebellion against that Creator. With the genetic and spiritual perfection of Adam and Eve and the flawless function of the environment that God had designed, man could have lived forever. That eternal state will once again be restored in the New Heavens and New Earth, but both man and the "ground" were sentenced to "death" by the Creator when Adam rebelled.

Something surely changed instantly in the Garden at the judgment. Adam and Eve "knew" they were without covering and ran to hide themselves from the sight of God. Perhaps, like the brilliance of the resurrected Christ that is revealed to us in the book of Revelation, Adam and Eve were "covered" with the glory of eternal life-force. Whatever instantaneous spiritual change took place within their bodies, the physical death that came upon the elements from which they were made was also a result of Adam's sin. That physical death merely reflected the withdrawal of the Creator's sustaining power. That death took a long time to overtake the majesty of God's "image" and the flawless design of the cosmos. But overtake, it did!

Later, after the terrible judgment of the global Flood, God reinstituted His sustaining and maintaining power back into the creation, promising, "While the earth remains, Seedtime and harvest, Cold and heat, Winter and summer, And day and night Shall not cease" (Genesis 8:22). Prior to God's gracious intervention, the horrible rebellion in the Garden started an exponential decline of physical properties and an awful increase in sinfulness in the hearts of men.

As the centuries progressed, the "thorns and the thistles" become more virulent, the "sweat" of work required becomes more onerous, and earth becomes "filled with violence" (Genesis 6:11). Man has health and long life to "subdue" and "have dominion." God's grace has allowed the cosmos to provide for his every need, yet "every intent of the thoughts" of man's heart "was only evil continually" (Genesis 6:5). Man's steward responsibility had degenerated into more and more evil behavior.

Time does not "cure all ills." Time reveals depravity.

Cain and Abel

The opening two verses of Genesis 4 document the birth of Cain and Abel. It seems clear that Cain was the firstborn, since Eve attaches such significance to his birth. Abel is probably the second child, although that is not specified. Adam and Eve had a plurality of "sons and daughters" (Genesis 5:4), but other than Cain, Abel, and Seth, the children are not named.

Jewish tradition claims that Adam and Eve bore some 60 children together. There is no reason to doubt such prolific reproduction. After all, the initial command from the Creator included the imperative to "multiply." It is likely they had many more than that, given their physical stamina, beauty, health, and longevity. One must remember, however, that the terse document of Adam's historical record skips many years between verses. Cain is, no doubt, born soon after the expulsion from the Garden; Abel, probably the following year. But when the events of Cain's sacrifice are introduced in verse 3, both Cain and Abel are adults.

The notation about the age of Adam at the birth of Seth (Genesis 4:3) indicates that the events recorded surrounding the disobedience of Cain and the subsequent murder of Abel took place more than a century after the creation. Seth is obviously intended to be the "replacement" for Abel, which would date the first human murder within the year before Seth's birth—probably 129 years after Adam and Eve had left the Garden.

Much would have happened during those years.

The sacrifice

The little phrase "in the process of time" which opens the scene to the sacrifice ceremony contains a significant piece of information. The Hebrew would best be translated "at the end of the days"—signifying a regular, repetitive, known time sequence that Adam and the growing population would have been familiar with. Although we are given the occupational talents of Cain as agricultural expert and Abel as a keeper of livestock, it makes no sense for them to suddenly appear in a formal ceremony with different sacrifices—especially given God's reaction to Cain's effort.

Please recall that God had made tunics of skin for Adam and Eve at the conclusion of the judgment as He cast them out of the Garden. That horrific scene would have been indelibly imprinted on their minds and hearts. They certainly watched as their Creator killed innocent animals in front of them, then skinned and prepared the coverings. Given the later institution of the annual "Day of Atonement," it is not at all presumptuous to expect God to demand that the human population observe some sort of formal sacrifice of animals in perpetuity until the "Lamb of God" finally came in future history.

It should be noted that such a formal animal sacrifice was not at all unknown or unusual. Noah offered animal sacrifices upon leaving the Ark. All of the patriarchs continued the practice. This, of course, is all prior to the Law and the codifying of the various sacrifices under Moses. Surely it does not do injustice to the brief information in Genesis 4 to infer that the sacrifice which preceded the judgment of Cain would have been a "regular" practice—probably an annual affair—and may well have been at the gate of the Garden under the watchful eyes of the Cherubim and the presence of the pre-incarnate Person of the Creator Himself.

Cain's disobedience

The sharp contrast between God's recognition of Abel's animal sacrifice and Cain's fruit offering is startling. The entire scene emphasizes that Cain's action was a sudden departure from years of accepted practice. Both Cain and Abel "came with" their sacrifice, indicating their intention to present it "to the LORD." The language used for Abel's offering is virtually identical to the phrases used by Moses as he iterates the requirements of God for the nation Israel.

> Abel also brought of the firstborn of his flock and of their fat. (Genesis 4:4)

> And unto the children of Israel thou shalt speak, saying, Take ye a kid of the goats for a sin offering; and a calf and a lamb, both of the first year, without blemish, for a burnt offering. (Leviticus 9:3)

It is therefore reasonable to infer that Abel brought what was expected and long practiced, and Cain, after following that precedent for all of his previous life, now chose to bring "an offering of the fruit of the ground to the LORD" (Genesis 4:3). Like his father before him, Cain clearly decided to disobey the demands of the Lord and bring something of his own work as sufficient. He knew what was expected of him. He had already experienced and participated in the worship. He willingly chose to dissent.

The Bible's own commentary on Cain's heart is important.

> Not as Cain who was of the wicked one and murdered his brother. And why did he murder him? Because his works were evil and his brother's righteous. (1 John 3:12)

> But these speak evil of whatever they do not know; and whatever they know naturally, like brute beasts, in these things they corrupt themselves. Woe to them! For they have gone in the way of Cain. (Jude 1:10-11)

Herein lies the core of all sin: conscious disobedience against God's authority.

God's mercy

Some have suggested that God's holiness is what God is. God's grace is His unmerited favor granted to those who do not deserve it. And God's mercy is God's judgment delayed on those who will not know His saving grace. If those short ideas are reasonably close to how God reveals Himself in the rest of Scripture, the interchange with Cain is surely a good example.

> And the LORD respected Abel and his offering, but He did not respect Cain and his offering. And Cain was very angry, and his countenance fell. So the LORD said to Cain, "Why are you angry? And why has your countenance fallen? If you do well, will you not be accepted? And if you do not do well, sin lies at the door. And its desire is for you, but you should rule over it." (Genesis 4:4-7)

The word choices in this short passage are significant. The "respect" shown to Abel and not to Cain implies much more than a mere recognition of correct behavior. The Hebrew word is *sha'ah*, most often translated "look." Given the implicit habitual sacrifice and the personal quotations from God Himself throughout the account, it is quite likely that the Lord, in the pre-incarnate manifestation of the second Person of the Godhead was present at these formal meetings, and "looked" at Abel while not "looking" at Cain. Such a personal rejection would have been obvious—and humiliating.

Cain lost it! Not only was he boiling with fury (the Hebrew words are as intense as can be expressed), but Cain's "countenance" collapsed. In simple terms, his face showed both the rage and the humiliation. This "man from the LORD" had become so enraged that everything about his manner and body language shrieked hostility.

Immediately, the Lord confronted Cain with a tender effort to reclaim him. So ever is our Lord. No matter how deliberate the sin, no matter how intense our anger at God, the gracious and merciful Creator seeks to restore the relationship. Cain had lived decades with evidence of God's constant care. Time and again Cain had come with his family to the altar of sacrifice and known the presence of God. There was no need or cause for Cain to "do his own thing" and yet the Lord "demonstrates His own love" (Romans 5:8) before the rage hardened into unrepentant sin and horrible consequence.

"Why are you angry? Why has your countenance fallen?" This gentle prodding could have—indeed should have—brought Cain around to his senses. Cain knew the rules. He knew that if he did what was expected by His Creator that he would be "accepted." The direct questions, then delivered by the Lord personally, are now delivered by the Holy Spirit, who "will convict the world of sin, and of righteousness, and of judgment" (John 16:8). The motivation is the same. God loves mankind, and is "not willing that any should perish but that all should come to repentance" (2 Peter 3:9).

But just as surely as the call and conviction goes out from God to bring repentance, so does the clear warning: "If you do not do well, sin lies at the door. And its desire is for you, but you should rule over it" (Genesis 4:7). These particular words to Cain should have triggered an undeniable memory in his mind. It is without doubt that Adam would have taught his children what God had commissioned them to do as stewards over earth. Mankind was to "have dominion" over the earth. Cain was warned that sin would "long" to possess him, but that he, Cain, should "have dominion" over it (same words).

No short interchange could have been more clear. But Cain refuses to respond.

Abel's murder

But no answer also means a "no" answer. Obviously, Cain turned away from God and went into the "field" to "talk" with Abel. The time element is not given, but it appears that the incident occurred shortly after his rejection at the formal sacrifice. Cain may have simmered and stewed for some time about the humiliation at the sacrifice, but this prototype of all murders involved anger and jealousy.

Now Cain talked with Abel his brother; and it came

to pass, when they were in the field, that Cain rose up
against Abel his brother and killed him. (Genesis 4:8)

The New Testament tells us that Abel was "righteous" and that
he had received the "witness" from God that he had offered a "more
excellent sacrifice" (Hebrews 11:4). Twice the Genesis text emphasizes that Abel was the "brother" of Cain. Everything would pressure
against any fell deed, but Cain "rose up" and murdered his brother.
How long Cain had been under the sway of Lucifer is not known.
The Scripture merely tells us that "his works were evil" (1 John 3:12).
Ultimately, such inclination and activities will produce the deeds that
will sear and bring final "condemnation" because men love "darkness
rather than light" (John 3:19).

Cain's denial

Once again, God seeks Cain out and confronts him with the horror of the sin.

Then the LORD said to Cain, "Where is Abel your brother?" He said, "I do not know. Am I my brother's keeper?"
(Genesis 4:9)

God always comes to us first. When sin occurs, we follow the pattern set by Adam and Eve and now repeated and intensified by Cain.
The first impulse is to run, hide, deny—anything but confess and
repent; but God *still* loves us. Any relationship with the Creator must
begin with His initial overture. "No one," the Lord Jesus would later
say, "can come to Me unless the Father who sent Me draws him" (John
6:44). So it is here with Cain.

Once again, Cain is given a chance to confess his sin and repent.
The simple question: "Where is your brother?" penetrates deep into
the heart and forces Cain to admit to himself what he has done. There
may be some sins that are committed in ignorance and naiveté, but
most of what we do is conscious and willfully done. Regret may come
(and usually does), but regret is not the same as repentance. Regret
senses the consequences to come and wants to avoid them. Repen-

tance abhors the deed and longs to correct it. Regret may wish that the event had not transpired and will usually embrace an excuse for the sin. Repentance recognizes the violation of righteousness and seeks the face of the One who can forgive.

Cain had a lot of regret, but no repentance.

The response of Cain to God's penetrating question gives insight into how quickly a human heart can harden. Adam and Eve gave excuses for their sin, but avoided open denial. Cain immediately throws his lie in the face of God and adds in flippant arrogance that he is not responsible for his brother's safety. Sin has moved from lying at the "door" of Cain's heart into a hostile takeover of Cain's actions and thoughts. This point of unalterable rebellion is both pathetic and horrible. The pathos of lives ruined is sad enough, but the future consequences of open sin are beyond contemplation. This sin ultimately resulted in world destruction. What an awful tragedy!

God's justice

> And He said, "What have you done? The voice of your brother's blood cries out to Me from the ground. So now you are cursed from the earth, which has opened its mouth to receive your brother's blood from your hand. When you till the ground, it shall no longer yield its strength to you. A fugitive and a vagabond you shall be on the earth." (Genesis 4:9-12)

Now the sovereign omniscience of God shatters the facade. "Be sure your sin will find you out," the Scripture warns (Numbers 32:23). God's knowledge penetrates our innermost thoughts and knows what our reactions will be. "For there is not a word on my tongue, But behold, O LORD, You know it altogether" (Psalm 139:2-4). God's Word penetrates "to the division of soul and spirit, and of joints and marrow, and is a discerner of the thoughts and intents of the heart" (Hebrews 4:12). No one *ever* gets away with their sin.

God's justice is swift and appropriate. Cain was a "tiller of the ground," which produce he proudly displayed in defiance of God's demand. Now the land that Cain had chosen to frame his life would no longer yield to his efforts. Cain had sought "respect" from God by his own standards. Now he would be a "fugitive and a vagabond," banished from the presence of the One he had sought to persuade. He had murdered his brother. Now Cain would fear that "anyone who finds me will kill me."

Sin seduces, but always, always destroys that which it suborns.

And even in judgment, God retains His own authority. Cain knew that his deed was so heinous that "anyone" would try to wreak vengeance on him for Abel's murder. However, God insists, "Vengeance is Mine, I will repay" (Romans 12:19). God will not alter or permit His holiness to be thwarted by any of His creation.

> Declaring the end from the beginning, And from ancient times things that are not yet done, Saying, "My counsel shall stand, And I will do all My pleasure," Calling a bird of prey from the east, The man who executes My counsel, from a far country. Indeed I have spoken it; I will also bring it to pass. I have purposed it; I will also do it. (Isaiah 46:10-11)

Whether a sparrow falls or the Dragon sets up an empire with minions fawning all over the plans for evil, God does not allow His will or pleasure to fail. Cain rightly feared for his life. God had reserved such retribution solely to Himself. Human passions and sinful hearts will always seek to execute their own version of retaliation, but only God is able to do so with utter holiness. God has delegated His "sword" to human governments as His agent (Genesis 9:6; Romans 13:4), but there has never been any hint in Scripture that personal vengeance or payback punishment is sanctioned.

> And the LORD said to him, "Therefore, whoever kills Cain, vengeance shall be taken on him sevenfold." And the LORD set a mark on Cain, lest anyone finding him should kill him. (Genesis 4:15)

Whatever this "mark" might have been, its purpose was to let all know that personal killing was not sanctioned. Many have suggested that God placed a visible "sign" on Cain that would be recognized whenever encountered. The word use in Scripture is very broad, describing everything from the widely visible token of the rainbow and the miracles of the ten plagues in Egypt to the private covenant of circumcision for the nation of Israel. But whatever this mark may have been, it was not inherited by Cain's descendants. This judgment and its protection applied to Cain alone.

Yes, God does note that sinful actions result in generations of consequence: "visiting the iniquity of the fathers upon the children and the children's children to the third and the fourth generation" (Exodus 34:7). The sin of one individual, however, is never transferred to another.

> "Behold, all souls are Mine; The soul of the father As well as the soul of the son is Mine; The soul who sins shall die." (Ezekiel 18:4)

> "The soul who sins shall die. The son shall not bear the guilt of the father, nor the father bear the guilt of the son. The righteousness of the righteous shall be upon himself, and the wickedness of the wicked shall be upon himself." (Ezekiel 18:20)

Cain's wife and city

This little notation in Scripture has aroused more questions than many more serious issues. Where did Cain get his wife?

> Then Cain went out from the presence of the LORD and dwelt in the land of Nod on the east of Eden. And Cain knew his wife, and she conceived and bore Enoch. And he built a city, and called the name of the city after the name of his son—Enoch. (Genesis 4:16-17)

Several important pieces of information are recorded by Adam in this section of his "book." God had decreed that Cain would be a "vagabond" for the rest of his life. The play on words is significant. The Hebrew word for "Nod" is essentially the same word as "vagabond." The term and its derivatives are used some 26 times in the Old Testament and are translated in various contexts as "wander" and "shake" to "wail" and "pity." Essentially the word means what would quickly be assumed: Cain was doomed to have no certain dwelling place for the rest of his life, in contrast to his love for the agricultural simplicity and stability.

Also, Adam notes that this land of wandering would be centralized "east of Eden." Interesting! This is precisely the same description for the location of the Garden (Genesis 2:8). Evidently, Cain tried his best to keep near the place where God might have previously met with him—even though Cain was driven from the "presence of the LORD."

Sad. Many a sinner tries in vain to restore the lost relationship and opportunities God had provided. Esau later regretted his hasty actions with Jacob and Isaac, but "found no place for repentance, though he sought it diligently with tears" (Hebrews 12:17).

Implicit in the worry expressed by Cain that he would be hunted and potentially killed by "anyone" is the drive to protect himself from such harm. Two observations are given in the text that pertain to this. First, Cain and his wife produce a son who is given the name Enoch. Then Cain builds a "city" and calls the place Enoch after his son. The questions arise: Where did the wife come from and where did the population come from to house a city?

Cain's family

Please remember that the murder of Abel took place at least a century after creation, more likely just before the birth of Seth when Adam had been alive for 130 years. The Hebrew language is a difficult language to gain tenses from the word structure. Much depends on the syntax and context of the passage. In this case, Cain's marriage and birth of an important son may have followed his expulsion, but could well be a statement of a previous condition resulting in a future consequence. That is, he could have married a "wife" many years before and would have had a growing family if such were the case.

Well, where would such a wife come from?

Obviously, Cain would have had to marry a sister or a niece. Genetic deformity would have been miniscule, if apparent at all. There was no restriction upon close marriage until Moses' time. God intended for the humanity to "multiply" in order for the earth to be properly cared for. Adam and Eve had "sons and daughters," and Genesis 4 lists six notable descendants from Cain's line. There is no reason not to expect proclivity in these pristine years, with geometric progression the norm rather than the exception.

Even very conservative assumptions suggest that the population after 125 years would be more than large enough for a "city" to be built and for Cain to choose and marry a "wife."

- There was no death until Abel's murder (125+ years, at least 5 generations)

- Assume a "marriage" or sexual partner engaged by age 25

- Allow for only 10 children from each pair: five boys, five girls

- After 125 years, the population would be at least 7,800

It doesn't take long to grow a population. This would have been especially true with the pristine environment and long lives of these first people. It is quite likely that the population would have been much larger. Very little is known about actual population rates during early recorded history. Average rates during more modern times have varied from 2 to 0.5 percent. Population models make assumptions, but even using death and marriage rates commensurate with modern history, an initial population of only two people, increasing at 2 percent per year, would become 3.5 billion people in only 1,075 years.

Cain would have chosen a partner from among the sisters, nieces, or subsequent grandchildren of the population, and Cain's children would have come quickly thereafter. Enoch may have been the first child, although that is not stated. Enoch was, apparently, the most favored of Cain's sons, and may well have figured prominently in the early plans of his father. Even if Cain did not marry until after his expulsion from the presence of the Lord, there would have been both ample time and ample population from which to marry, start a family, and build a "city."

This "city" may well have been only a fortification for purposes of protection from assumed attack. The term is widely used in the Old Testament to label everything from a collection of tents to a population center. Given the judgment from God on Cain, it is likely that he and his growing family built some sort of walled enclosure that would house them in the event of an attack by presumed enemies. Over time, the fortification would have probably become more similar to the extended villages that we tend to associate with such places, but there really is no way to know what was built "east of Eden."

It is possible Cain thought he could re-create the Garden from which his family was banished; he no doubt had heard the Garden described by his parents, and perhaps he was able to get a glimpse of the Garden through its gate. Perhaps, given that he was forced to "wander" as a "fugitive" for the rest of his life, he tried to build a secure place for his extended family to live. Since the "land" would no longer "yield her strength" to Cain, he may well have attempted to establish some sort of trading post from which to barter services or knowledge to others. None of this is recorded, but all of this is immanently possible. There were more than enough people and more than enough time for everything that is recorded in the text to be accurately portrayed.

Lamech and Enoch

Both Lamech and Enoch, whose records are established in Genesis 4-5, are in the seventh recorded generation from Adam. The names listed may be the more notable of each generation rather than first sons, but there is no evidence that the lists are anything except a sequential record of the heads of each generation. Cain's line does not give the ages at birth or death, but the parallel table given in chapter 5 of Adam's descendants is given in such precision that we can identify the time in which they lived after the creation week.

Assuming that each generation roughly parallels the other, Lamech and Enoch lived during the same era, certainly occurring over several centuries together. Enoch's birth occurs 622 years after creation (simple event-to-event math). Since both he and Lamech are cited as opposite examples of lifestyles and both are the seventh generation through their respective lines, we can surely conclude that they were alive during the same period.

Enoch is one of two in Scripture who are said to have been taken up into heaven without death (Enoch, Hebrews 11:5; Elijah, 2 Kings 2:11). That event is recorded as taking place when Enoch was 365 years old (Genesis 5:23-24), making the common time of Lamech and Enoch between 622 and 987 years after creation. Their lives overlapped for some 350 years during the "Middle Ages" of the pre-Flood world. God has caused their lives to be noted in Scripture to give us some insight into the progression of civilization and the diametric opposition that these different lines came to represent.

The line of Cain

Many of Cain's descendants had, no doubt, followed their first father's rebellion. The centuries passed, and there is nothing noted about the major sons until we get to Lamech. If he is representative of the line, as seems to be the purpose of giving the information, then Cain's line has degenerated into open rebellion as well as obvious prosperity.

Two wives are identified for Lamech. There is no indication that they were forced into this relationship, and every expectation that they willingly married him. Both are identified by name. Adah means "ornament" and Zillah means "shade." The names may well give us some insight into their beauty, and perhaps the reason that Lamech brought them into his household.

But the significant element in this portion of the record is that Lamech is the first one identified who openly defied God's initial commandment for monogamy. There is absolutely no indication that such a dual partnering had gone on before, and this was such an open rejection of the specific pattern designed by God that it became "famous" in the history of Cain. Later others would "choose" many daughters for themselves and attempt to raise "renown" for their names. Lamech, apparently, led the way into this debauchery.

Four notable children are born through the two wives of Lamech. Jabal is recognized as one who organized cattle-raising and tent-dwelling nomads, probably following the wandering of his long-ago father. Jubal, Jabal's brother, was an inventor of musical instruments, perhaps attempting to ease the burden of the "fugitive" worry of the family line. Tubalcain became renowned as an "instructor" of every sort of metallurgy. The alloy of brass required knowledge of both mining and the smelting of the compound ores. Naamah, the daughter of Zillah and sister of Tubalcain, may well have been noted for her personality. Her name means "pleasant."

Lamech also is noted for his arrogance and braggadocios in the murder of a man who had hurt him in some way. Perhaps this was a prelude to the "violence" that would consume mankind in the centuries to follow. What is noteworthy, however, is the flagrant and unashamed "voice" (sound, thunder) of his deed.

> Then Lamech said to his wives: "Adah and Zillah, hear my voice; Wives of Lamech, listen to my speech! For I have killed a man for wounding me, Even a young man for hurting me. If Cain shall be avenged sevenfold, Then Lamech seventy-sevenfold." (Genesis 4:23-24)

Once again, the lingering impact of Cain is felt. Lamech repeats the promise of God for Cain and brags that he is far more worthy of life than Cain could ever be. If God would avenge the death of Cain seven times, Lamech would avenge any "wounding" to him seventy seven times. The fearful regret expressed by Cain has been replaced by dangerous arrogance.

There is absolutely no evidence of a "religious" side to Lamech. His faith is in himself. He believed that he could do anything he pleased—and so he did. He believed in personal revenge and took it. He believed that he was more important than God and said so. Lamech was wrong and had chosen foolishly to defy the God of creation, but he was not a hypocrite.

The line of Seth

The last two verses of Genesis 4 introduce the line of Adam through Seth. Seth was born in the 130th year of Adam's life, and was the son born right after the murder of Abel. The list that follows seems to suggest that these people try to follow the instructions of God and make a worship of the Creator central to their culture.

> And Adam knew his wife again, and she bore a son and named him Seth, "For God has appointed another seed for me instead of Abel, whom Cain killed." And as for Seth, to him also a son was born; and he named him Enosh. Then men began to call on the name of the LORD. (Genesis 4:25-26)

It is clear that Adam and Eve considered Seth the replacement for Abel, and expected him to fulfill the role that had been so violently destroyed by Cain. Cain and his families had left the area, moving into the "land of Nod" on the east side of Eden. Adam's family, apparently, was separated from regular interchange with the heirs of Cain, and began to establish a more formal distance both in location and in lifestyle.

Seth's primary son, Enos, born when Seth was 105 years old, became a leader in some notable way when "men began to call on the name of the LORD." The population has now been growing for over 250 years and would have numbered well into the thousands. Although there was as yet no recognition of what we might think of as a government, the numbers of family groups and growing commerce would have necessitated some form of community interchange. With Cain and descendants off away eastward, the Adamic family, under the leadership of Seth and Enos, "began to call upon the name of the LORD."

That specific phrase is used only six times in all of Scripture. Perhaps a quick review of the citations would be helpful for a better understanding of what is meant by the words.

> And to Seth, to him also there was born a son; and he called his name Enos: then began men to *call upon the name of the LORD*. (Genesis 4:26)

> I will take the cup of salvation, and *call upon the name of the LORD*. (Psalm 116:13)

> I will offer to thee the sacrifice of thanksgiving, and will *call upon the name of the LORD*. (Psalm 116:17)

> For then will I turn to the people a pure language, that they may all *call upon the name of the LORD, to serve him* with one consent. (Zephaniah 3:9)

> For whosoever shall *call upon the name of the Lord* shall be saved. (Romans 10:13)

> Unto the church of God which is at Corinth, to them that are sanctified in Christ Jesus, called to be saints, with all that in every place *call upon the name of Jesus Christ our Lord*, both theirs and ours: (1 Corinthians 1:2)

It can be quickly seen that each time the phrase is used, there is some form of worship identified; most of the worship described is public and structured. Whatever may have been the format in Seth's time, the Scripture found it important to note that it was after the death of Abel that the population developing through the line of Adam, Seth, and Enos became more focused in their worship of the Creator. Perhaps some form of "rest day" observance was coupled with a more formal focus on the person and worship of God. Whatever may have been the case, this was in direct contrast with the growing distance between the people of Seth and the people of Cain. And so it has ever been.

"If the world hates you, you know that it hated Me before it hated you. If you were of the world, the world would love its own. Yet because you are not of the world, but I chose you out of the world, therefore the world hates you. Remember the word that I said to you, 'A servant is not greater than his master.' If they persecuted Me, they will also persecute you. If they kept My word, they will keep yours also." (John 15:18-20)

Enoch is the one who becomes the pinnacle of righteous behavior and love for the walk in holiness before his Creator. Remember, Enoch and Lamech of Cain's line live at approximately the same time, and they are chosen to give the contrasting pictures of the "godly" and the "ungodly." Enoch seems chosen by God to be both an unsullied example of godliness and a unique vessel for extraordinary service.

And Enoch walked with God: and he was not; for God took him. (Genesis 5:24)

By faith Enoch was translated that he should not see death; and was not found, because God had translated him: for before his translation he had this testimony, that he pleased God. (Hebrews 11:5)

Some have suggested that Enoch will be one of the "Two Witnesses" during the Tribulation events who will openly resist the Antichrist. Elijah was the other Old Testament prophet who was taken directly into heaven without going through death. This is surely plausible, but the totality of their witness and unique purpose in life is not revealed in Scripture.

And Enoch also, the seventh from Adam, prophesied of these, saying, Behold, the Lord cometh with ten thousands of his saints. (Jude 1:14)

This little cameo in the book of Jude is quite interesting. Enoch, living through 350 years during the first age of the earth, was prophesying about the Second Coming of Christ! What a contrast. Cain's Lamech was bragging about his murder of retribution and how much more important he was than Cain. Enoch is walking with God and preaching about the Second Coming!

This period of time was right in the middle of the First Age before the destruction by the great Flood during Noah's day. From this point on, over the next 700 years, the population of earth begins to degenerate. By the time Adam and Seth were dead, Enoch had been taken up into heaven, and Noah was in his prime, the world was totally corrupt.

> Then the LORD saw that the wickedness of man was great in the earth, and that every intent of the thoughts of his heart was only evil continually. And the LORD was sorry that He had made man on the earth, and He was grieved in His heart. (Genesis 6:5-6)

> The earth also was corrupt before God, and the earth was filled with violence. So God looked upon the earth, and indeed it was corrupt; for all flesh had corrupted their way on the earth. (Genesis 6:11-12)

The apostle Peter tells us that the world that existed then was totally destroyed by a *cataklysmos*, a cataclysm of water that entirely eradicated what was. Our *cosmos* today is very different. Scarred and marred by the upheaval of the earth's destruction, we can only glimpse what might have been through the record of the first six chapters of Genesis and the enormous burial grounds of the fossil record.

What caused God to be so angry? How can we understand the justification for the enormous destruction of billions of people and nearly all air-breathing life? There is much we can learn. We will discuss it in the next chapter.

CHAPTER TEN
THE END OF THE AGE

The First Age of the earth is actually not very long. A straight event-to-event addition of the dates given in Genesis 4-5 indicate that the entire history spans little more than 1,656 years. As has been noted, this entire section of history is covered in six chapters. Obviously, the information provided by the God of creation is very selective. Details are provided for the creation week, certain events on Day Six of creation, a few hours that outline the temptation and fall of humanity, a murder over a century later, and a cameo about two key lives during the seventh generation of humanity.

Finally, we are given a list of the dates and ages of the main leaders of Adam's line through Seth, a summary description of the final 120 years before the flood, and a more detailed analysis of God's call of Noah and the building of the Ark to preserve life on the earth. Perhaps a table of those key lives would be helpful to understand the relationship between the main heads of the families.

Pre-Flood Patriarchs

Patriarch	Year of Birth after Creation	Age at Birth of Next Patriarch	Year of Death
Adam	1	130	930
Seth	130	105	1042
Enos	235	90	1140
Cainan	325	70	1235
Mahalaleel	395	65	1290
Jared	460	162	1422
Enoch	622	65	987*
Methuselah	687	187	1656**
Lamech	874	182	1651
Noah	1056	500	2006

* Enoch was translated to heaven without dying
** Methuselah died the year the Flood came

There is absolutely no internal evidence to view these records as anything but accurate history—other than a refusal to accept the records as history. The records are given just as one would expect for a historical record. And except for the long lives, which have been dealt with in the text and by the very purpose of the Creator, there is nothing unusual about the record. These names are listed again in 1 Chronicles 1:1-4 and Luke 3:36-38, verifying that the writers of both the Old and New Testaments accepted the Genesis genealogies as historical fact.

Significance of the Names

Much could be said about the naming of the key family leaders of both of the lines of Seth and Cain. Studies of all ancient cultures have confirmed that names bore much more significance than they do in modern societies. Names were given to represent something about the person's character or that would identify the events during which the person was born. Although the Hebrew etymology of the names is somewhat difficult to pin down, the table below gives a fairly good representation of the ideas behind the names.

Seth	"Appointed One"
Enos	"Mortal Frailty"
Cainan	"Smith"
Mahalaleel	"God Be Praised"
Jared	"Descent"
Enoch	"Dedication"
Methuselah	"When He Dies, Judgment"
Lamech	"Conqueror"
Noah	"Rest" or "Comfort"

A quick look back in Genesis 4 at Cain's genealogies show two names that are the same. Enoch and Lamech pop out immediately, suggesting to some that there was a copycat or an overlap in the genealogies. Actually, both lines named these important heirs in very different periods. Although the names are the same with a very similar etymology, the emphasis was quite different. The Enoch of Cain was "dedicated" to preserving the line and withstanding the judgment of God. The Enoch of Seth was "dedicated" to the service of God and was known for his godly walk and prophetic ministry. The Lamech of Cain boasted that he was a "conqueror" of anyone who would dare to defy him. The Lamech of Seth looked to "conquer" the ungodliness that was growing around him, even naming his son expecting the "rest" or "comfort" that God had promised through his grandfather, Enoch.

Same names. Vastly different perspectives.

The World Before the Flood

Modern evolutionary thought has so pervaded education and media that it is almost impossible to imagine ancient times without a vision of cavemen, raw meat, clubs, primitive conditions, and raging ecologies. Every documentary shown and lecture given seems to start with the mantra "millions of years ago." Because of education's evolutionary indoctrination, it is almost impossible to imagine where the knowledge came from to build the vast pyramids in Egypt or account for the technology of the Aztecs.

And because most modern scholars and historians reject the biblical information outright, explanations are as widely varied as visiting space men with gravity-defying rays or hand labor by millions of slaves. It is just assumed that the "ancient" civilizations were still evolving from tree-hugging, knuckle-dragging hominids and would hardly have had time to develop "sophisticated" knowledge to build vast edifices and complex societies.

The Bible tells a very different story.

Superior intelligence

Not only were Adam and Eve created personally by an omniscient Being, but they were pronounced "very good" by a holy, omnipotent, loving, and enteral Creator. The intelligence of those flawless humans would have been far superior to what any "genius" would possess today.

In a single afternoon, Adam was able to evaluate and name all of the kinds of cattle and beasts of the field that God caused to be brought before him in the Garden. With perceptions that we can only envy, the shapes, actions, and characteristics of each animal were seen, processed, and identified. Many of those names still linger in literature and lore.

Communication skills

Contrary to common ideas, the first humans did not grunt and squeak, nor bang out their passions on cave walls and the heads of others; they possessed language and writing skills from the earliest moments. Adam's "book" (Genesis 5:1) was the foundational record for the early chapters of Genesis, and the rest of Seth's line wrote records to preserve the pertinent data for the remainder of time.

Conversations are recorded of the earliest interchanges involving Adam, Eve, Cain, Abel, Enoch, Lamech, etc. And these conversations are not the instinctive reactions of body language with grunts for emphasis, but dialogues with logic, questions, evasive answers, deductive conclusions, and other evidences of critical thinking. These were not beetle-browed, mumbling and bumbling, barely sentient beings. These men and women bore the image of their Creator—they *knew* Him.

May shame embarrass the Christian who still views these early people as mud-covered, cave-dwelling, morose and taciturn dimwits who waddled in ignorance. The Bible presents them as brilliant and beautiful, fully capable and fully aware "stewards" of earth.

Cities and commerce

The first recorded "city" is built in the second century of earth's history. There may well have been others. Population grew geometrically during those years, and it is surely plausible that various gatherings of family groups would have developed systems of housing and protection.

Abel was a "keeper" of cattle. Cain had developed systems for growing the crops necessary for feeding the increasing population. The idea of a "hunter-gather" is nothing more than evolutionary imagination built on the atheistic dogma of slow development over ages of environmentally driven "selection." There is absolutely no such concept in the Scriptures.

By the time seven centuries had passed, most of the tens of thousands of people were still alive, and the account in Genesis 4 of Lamech's talented children records a vast network of commerce in agriculture and metallurgy. The similarity of names in the two main genealogies indicate that there was communication between the groups, and that would certainly necessitate some form of commerce and travel. Even the fine arts developed to the point where complex musical instruments are developed and their master artificer is renowned for his skill.

Remember that these people all lived for hundreds of years. The ability to gain knowledge and perfect skills and efficiencies are only now being mimicked by our ability to store and retrieve information through computing power and rather instantaneous transfer of data. And please note that such power has barely been developed during the past 100 years and is just now becoming widely available.

Geometric growth

World reproduction rates, as measured today, indicate that most children are born by the time the parents reach age 25, with family sizes reaching stability by the time the parents are 35. Family size varies by country and culture, with some cultures encouraging large families and others trying to reduce population by limiting the reproduction rates to two children (replacement) or fewer. World population is growing, however, which means that the overall rate is more than two, and probably closer to four children per reproductive pair. Thus, a generation would be 35 years and our present world population of six-plus billion could be achieved from Noah's three sons and their wives in a little over 1,000 years.

Obviously, wars and plagues take their toll over time, so the long-term rates of reproduction during recorded history is probably closer to the famous 2.5 children per family. What is glaringly clear, however, is that the human population could not have been growing for anything like a million years. There is not enough space on the planet to hold that kind of population—even with a population growth rate of 0.25 percent!

Prior to the great Flood at the end of this first age, men lived to great ages and apparently had large families. Repeated often in the lists of Genesis 4-5 is the notation that each named generation head had "sons and daughters," making a minimal family of two sons and two daughters. The reality was probably much greater. Other than Enoch, who was taken to heaven without going through death, the average longevity of these pre-Flood peoples was 912 years! Recorded ages at the births of the various children ranged from 65 years to 500 years.

The pre-Flood world, nonetheless, would have seen fast growth. Families were large and lives were long. If one uses a very conservative formula of six children for each family, an average generation of 100 years, and a lifespan of 500 years, there would have been over 235 million people alive at the time of the global Flood. That is probably much too low an estimate. For instance, if the average family size were eight instead of six, and the generation was only 93 instead of 100, then the population at the death of Adam (930 years after creation) would have been 2.8 million. At that rate, the population at the time of the Flood would have been over 137 billion![1]

No one knows, of course, what the actual population would have been. But it is easily understood that the human population would have grown exponentially under the most conservative of calculations. Obviously there would have no problem for Cain to find a wife or build a city. And, more importantly, the Flood that God sent to destroy "all life" would have to have been global in extent to accomplish that end.

Growing Wickedness

The opening text of Genesis 6 appears to move from the braggadocios polygamy of Lamech in Genesis 4.

> Now it came to pass, when men began to multiply on the face of the earth, and daughters were born to them, that the sons of God saw the daughters of men, that they were beautiful; and they took wives for themselves of all whom they chose. (Genesis 6:1-2)

1   Henry Morris, 1970, *Biblical Cosmology and Modern Science,* Grand Rapids, MI: Baker Books, 87.

Lamech is the first man in world history to be identified as bringing two women into his home in direct defiance of what God had established at the time of creation. Lamech and his family lived and prospered in the seventh century after creation and may well have been alive when the practice of polygamy became commonplace, as recorded in Genesis 6:1-2. Several times "violence" is expressed as the end product of the world peoples moving ever further away from the "good" that God had designed and intended that the universe should be.

Almost a millennium passed since the early lives of Lamench and Enoch as recorded in Genesis 4 until the sad comments of God noted in Genesis 6. The wickedness of humanity had become "great" and the lifestyle of earth's population had become "corrupt."

So God finally responded:

> "My Spirit shall not strive with man forever, for he is indeed flesh; yet his days shall be one hundred and twenty years." (Genesis 6:3).

Several commentators have tried to explain away the common reading of this passage. Some have suggested, since it is obvious that the long lives of these pre-Flood men were not what they appear to be in simple language (i.e., they could not have lived for hundreds of years), that God is merely indicating that He is ready to bring judgment on humanity. But why the specific time? Why 120 years? That makes no sense unless it is recorded to give us the remaining time until the flood judgment will come on the earth.

Some others have suggested that God is dictating that from this point onward, the average lifespan would be 120 years. Once again, there is no such evidence that supports that. Noah's children and their children's children lived many centuries. It wasn't until the time of Moses that "normal" lifespans came anywhere near 120 years. No, this emphatic statement by God specifies that He, the Creator, was giving man only 120 years more until He, the God and the Judge of all things, would bring an end to this world.

Before that 120 years had elapsed, the horror of sinful rebellion had increased so much that "the wickedness of man was great in the earth, and that every intent of the thoughts of his heart was only evil continually" (Genesis 6:5). And even as God's own heart ached at the foolishness of His crowning creation grasping after every nuance of the knowledge of evil, earth became "corrupt before God, and the earth was filled with violence....Indeed it was corrupt; for all flesh had corrupted their way on the earth" (Genesis 6:11-12).

What a pitiful sight. Everything "good" had been provided. The whole earth was before them with liberty to learn, explore, and develop all that would enhance their lives for wonder and joy. Yet, the whole population only sought for evil all the time.

The Giants

> There were giants on the earth in those days, and also af-
> terward, when the sons of God came in to the daughters
> of men and they bore children to them. Those were the
> mighty men who were of old, men of renown. (Genesis
> 6:4)

The word "giants" is a translation of the Hebrew word *nephal*, with the plural *nephalim*. It is used only three times in the Old Testament, once here in Genesis 6:4, and twice in Numbers 13:33 telling of the "giants" that the 12 spies of Israel encountered when they went into the borders of Canaan to determine what lay in front of them as they prepared for war on the western side of the Jordan.

Nephal is rooted in the more common word *naphal*, which means "to fall." All of the Hebrew lexicons give the basic connotation of both words as "the fallen ones." Size is not inherent in the word *nephalim*, although that image was assumed in the story told by the 10 spies when they came back terrified, having seen some men who made them feel like "grasshoppers" as they spied on Canaan (Numbers 13:33).

Gigantism is certainly not unknown in human history. In recent history, various giants have made notoriety in the *Guinness Book of*

Records. Robert Wadlow is listed as the tallest person for whom there is irrefutable medical evidence, at 8 feet 11.1 inches. He was called the "Alton Giant" because his hometown was Alton, Illinois. Zeng Jinlian is one of 14 females who reached a height of 8 feet or more. She was 8 feet 1.75 inches tall. Professional basketball players are all enormous by "regular" standards, many of whom are well over 7 feet tall. And who can forget Goliath the Philistine of Gath? According to Scripture, he was "nine cubits and a span" (1 Samuel 17:4). The length of a "cubit" is still in debate, but if 18 inches is the accepted length, and a "span" is about 6 inches, then Goliath was about 14 feet tall! That *is* big!

All this to demonstrate that "giants" are not miraculous. They are, indeed, unusual in the human population, but are certainly not unheard of. What then, makes these "giants" in Genesis more noteworthy than others throughout history? Perhaps it is the implication that they were the result of some selective breeding with the "sons of God" and the "daughters of men."

The sons of God

The Hebrew phrase *bene elohim* appears twice in Genesis and three times in Job. All the references in Job are clearly talking about angelic creatures (Job 1:6; 2:1; 38:7). There is no evidence anywhere else in the Old Testament to take this phrase any other way than referencing angels. Thus, when the phrase is used in Genesis 6, one must assume that the primary reference is to angelic beings.

Some have suggested that this phrase is an attempt to recognize the godly line of Seth, Adam's "replacement" son for Abel. There is no reason or evidence in the text of Scripture to do so, however, other than to attempt to get around the problem of angels being able to procreate with humanity. Twice-born saints have made the tragic mistake of marrying an unbeliever. The result may well be awful, but never does some sort of supernatural "giant" result from such a union. There is nothing supernatural about good people making the wrong choice. That happens all too often.

If, however, angelic beings could couple with humanity and produce some sort of hybrid demigod, that would be a real problem.

Angels can and do assume the form of men, and do so in such a convincing manner that they were sought for homosexual partnering by the men of Sodom (Genesis 19:4-5). Whenever they appear throughout other times in the biblical narrative, they always appear as men, never as women, and always their appearance is stunning! They appear as a human in form, but there is no mistaking that they are more than mere men (Genesis 32:24; Daniel 3:25; Daniel 9:21; Luke 1:19; Luke 24:4, etc.).

While there is no specific passage that precludes angelic beings from sexual activity when they are in temporary human form, the Lord Jesus clearly states that the human ability bound up in marriage and the "one flesh" that comes from that union is not given to angels (Matthew 22:30 and Mark 12:25). Since angelic beings are "spirit" creatures and humans are "fleshly" creatures, there is no possibility that these two entirely different "kinds" could be inter-fertile and produce some sort of demigod, a hybrid flesh-spirit creature.

All creation was restricted within reproduction to "after its kind" (Genesis 1:11-12, 21, 24-25). This universal limitation was noted by the Lord Jesus to illustrate the inability of fruit trees to produce anything other than what their design permitted them to do (Luke 6:43-44). Later, the apostle Paul summarized the necessity of the resurrection, which must supernaturally change the "mortal" to the immortal, since all of creation from stars and angels to the most simple of life on earth cannot cross the "kind" from which they are made (1 Corinthians 15:38-54).

The trouble obviously surfaces with Genesis 6 when these "sons of God" were said specifically to produce "men of renown" through sexual union with the daughters of men. Whatever was going on, it appears that angels were involved. It also seems that the angelic induced offspring were "giants" and that this had been going on for some time, to the point that these "giants" became "mighty men" who had been "of old" and that they were "men of renown." Lots of descriptive information in that short little verse. Perhaps a quick analysis can help flesh out the record.

Men of renown

> ...when the sons of God came in to the daughters of men
> and they bore children to them. Those were the mighty
> men who were of old, men of renown. (Genesis 6:4)

Apparently there is something unusual about this developing union between the "sons of God" and the "daughters of men" that brings about a significant rise in wickedness and a power over the population, and in turn causes God to decide to destroy the earth and everything that has breath in it. Whatever happened, earth history since the end of the Flood knows nothing like that awful time.

There are some clues, however.

To begin with, these "sons of God" were selecting women from among the growing population—probably from among those with both long life histories and physical prowess. Hence the Bible notes: "they took wives for themselves of all whom they chose" (Genesis 6:2). Such selective breeding programs are not unknown in history. The 20th century is stained with the brothels of Hitler trying to raise up a "master" race while he was attempting to exterminate the "unfit" Jews. Nearly all of human history groans with the efforts of kings and bishops riding high on the backs of the "sheep" of their people while inter-marrying and despotically manipulating the affairs of wealth and politics to their advantage.

Lucifer's plan from the beginning was to take over the Throne of creation from the Creator. The Bible gives many details and broad prophecies that show the attempts over the ages to bring about an army of humanity that would be large enough and strong enough to defeat the "host" of heaven. Why should we be surprised to see such an attempt in the early chapters of Genesis?

These "mighty" men and the men of "renown" are nothing more

than Lucifer's manipulation of humanity, growing both in numbers and in wickedness, to bring about a rebellion against heaven. The word choices bear that out. The "might" of these selectively bred men emphasizes physical prowess—even military cunning. The "renown" they hold is nothing more than a "name," a "reputation" that fits with their deeds.

Shortly after the Flood, Nimrod would arise among the population at Babel, leading the people in a similar rebellion. Legends and stories abound of such "mighty men" who have "saved" tribes, villages, cities, and nations through various heroic deeds. These stories all have similar genres and all carry the message that some "great" person will rise up to rescue troubled humanity with near supernatural powers. Read the Bible's warnings about the Antichrist and the False Prophet.

Wise King Solomon observed, "That which has been is what will be, That which is done is what will be done, And there is nothing new under the sun" (Ecclesiastes 1:9).

Demonic control or possession

The resolution to the difficulties of this passage becomes clear. These "sons of God" must be angelic creatures. There is nothing in the Bible language to permit another application. The "daughters of men" can only be human. There is nothing that would indicate otherwise. The unusual result of the selective breeding is significant. Normal sexual unions in a random population, unless selected and controlled by careful thought, would not produce "mighty" or "renown" offspring.

Since the angelic beings are of a different "kind" than men, and since sexual reproduction under normal genetic processes would not produce any unusually powerful or highly trained beings, the only solution remaining is that angelic beings, with their greater knowledge and abilities to control wicked men, would possess and select both the men and the women necessary to build a "master race" that would suit Lucifer's design of rebellion and usurpation.

Good men having sex with several ungodly women would not

accomplish this. Angelic beings could not reproduce with another "kind" of being. Genetic knowledge would be available to angelic beings, but not necessarily to men. Violence and perversion seems to be the objective of the "whole earth," with every thought being evil all the time. Ultimate renown seems to be the desire of Lucifer and those who follow him.

Imprisoned angels

It is important to note that the Bible gives several references to an event in the past that was so awful and so devastating that those angels who participated in those times were thrown into a unique prison and will not participate in the affairs of this world until the end of the final age.

> He [Jesus] went and preached to the spirits in prison, who formerly were disobedient, when once the Divine longsuffering waited in the days of Noah, while the ark was being prepared, in which a few, that is, eight souls, were saved through water. (1 Peter 3:19-20)

> For if God did not spare the angels who sinned, but cast them down to hell and delivered them into chains of darkness, to be reserved for judgment; and did not spare the ancient world, but saved Noah, one of eight people, a preacher of righteousness, bringing in the flood on the world of the ungodly. (2 Peter 2:4-5)

> And the angels who did not keep their proper domain, but left their own abode, He has reserved in everlasting chains under darkness for the judgment of the great day. (Jude 1:6)

Both of the references in Peter are obviously speaking about an event that took place during the time that Noah was preparing the Ark which would rescue eight people and sufficient animal kind to start life anew after the Flood. Those angels were cast into *tartaroo*, a unique Greek word only used in 2 Peter 2:4, which apparently signifies the deepest recesses of Sheol where the spirits the dead are kept.

Lots of mystery here, but when Jude speaks of angels who refused to keep their "proper domain" and were cast into "everlasting chains" as a result, the overall message seems to share a common theme.

Angelic beings were charged with ministering to those who would become the heirs of salvation (Hebrews 1:14). Those who apparently sided with Lucifer in his rebellion against the Creator became involved (prior to the building of the Ark) with a plot to suborn and manipulate the development of humanity into "men of renown" who might overthrow all that the Creator had done. Their partial success brought about the destruction of the world. Their own participation in those horrific deeds brought about their own imprisonment "under darkness" until the "great day" of God's return and the restoration of the new heaven and new earth.

Noah Found Grace

Genesis 6:8 is the first time the word "grace" appears in the Bible. Right there, in the midst of the most awful social evil and demonic rebellion that world will ever know until the last great rebellion just before the utter meltdown of the universe, Noah "found grace in the eyes of the LORD."

The world is in turmoil. The Nephalim are rising into power. Demonic evil is manipulating the people. The whole earth is filled with violence. Noah, however, "was a just man, perfect in his generations. Noah walked with God" (Genesis 6:9). It is hard to imagine a more stressful and confusing time for a man who sought to understand what was happening. Noah lives a "righteous" life in the midst of this terrible wicked violence. Noah is "without blemish" among the inhabitants, yet his influence is, apparently, having no impact.

But Noah found grace in the eyes of the Lord.

That simple statement should give all of us hope and confidence in what God is doing. If you have not yet felt alone or troubled or useless among those in your circle, you will. Ordinary circumstances do not often appear to tip toward God's side. The "bad guys" seem to win more often than not. But "grace" is always just around the corner in God's omniscient eye.

> Do not fret because of evildoers, nor be envious of the workers of iniquity. For they shall soon be cut down like the grass, and wither as the green herb. Trust in the LORD, and do good; dwell in the land, and feed on His faithfulness. Delight yourself also in the LORD, and He shall give you the desires of your heart. Commit your way to the LORD, trust also in Him, and He shall bring it to pass. (Psalm 37:1-5)

Noah surely would have seen the awful wickedness and violence that permeated the land. No doubt he was frustrated because those he had any contact with "were eating and drinking, marrying and giving in marriage" (Matthew 24:38) as though nothing was the matter. But God had another plan—beyond the mindset of the wicked and beyond the imagination of Noah.

The Ark

> And God said to Noah, "The end of all flesh has come before Me, for the earth is filled with violence through them; and behold, I will destroy them with the earth. Make yourself an ark of gopherwood; make rooms in the ark, and cover it inside and outside with pitch. And this is how you shall make it: The length of the ark shall be three hundred cubits, its width fifty cubits, and its height thirty cubits. You shall make a window for the ark, and you shall finish it to a cubit from above; and set the door of the ark in its side. You shall make it with lower, second, and third decks. And behold, I Myself am bringing floodwaters on the earth, to destroy from under heaven all flesh in which is the breath of life; everything that is on the earth shall die. (Genesis 6:13-17)

This is one big box! You may remember that the ordinary hydrological cycle that we are familiar with today was unknown during the

228

First Age after creation. God had prepared a system of "mist" (perhaps like modern geysers) that watered the entire globe at night (Genesis 2:6). Whether or not this system was still in operation 1,600 years or so after creation is not affirmed, but the idea of building a watertight Ark would have been startling, to say the least!

And this thing was big! Scholars are still fussing over what the "cubit" measured, but we can assume that it would have been around 18 inches. That means that the Ark would have been at least 450 feet long, 75 feet wide, and 45 feet high. That is bigger than any seagoing vessel ever built until the 1800s. It was built with three decks containing over 1,400,000 cubic feet of space, more than enough space to house 100,000 animals, along with whatever food may have been needed for the duration.

Many have scoffed at the idea of God preserving life through the Ark. Some have suggested that there are over 1,000,000 species of animals. That is true, by man's definition of species, but God was only interested in preserving the different "kinds" of life—and only that life that lived or flew on or above the land. No aquatic life was included—and that accounts for nearly 800,000 of the species according to human taxonomy. The remaining land and air creatures were to be two of every "kind" with seven of the "clean" animal kind.

Kind, as the reader will remember from chapter 5 and 6 of this book, were probably more near the "family" or "genus" of the modern classification. Only two "dog kind" would have been taken instead of the many "species" of dog (mostly man-made, by the way). The same would be true for the "beasts of the earth" and the "fowl of the air." Just where the "kind" begins and stops no one yet knows for sure, but it is certain that they would have represented far fewer than the 200,000 or so remaining land and air "species" of our modern thought.

And most animals are rather small. The average size is something like a sheep, with many being much smaller. The few large animals (elephants, giraffe, cattle, dinosaurs, etc.) would have been selected for their reproducing ability—in their animal teens or young adult stages, rather than the old and largest specimen. The Ark would have had plenty of room to house the 50,000 or so creatures "to keep the species alive on the face of all the earth" (Genesis 7:3).

The Covenant

> But I will establish My covenant with you; and you shall go into the ark—you, your sons, your wife, and your sons' wives with you. And of every living thing of all flesh you shall bring two of every sort into the ark, to keep them alive with you; they shall be male and female. Of the birds after their kind, of animals after their kind, and of every creeping thing of the earth after its kind, two of every kind will come to you to keep them alive. And you shall take for yourself of all food that is eaten, and you shall gather it to yourself; and it shall be food for you and for them. Thus Noah did; according to all that God commanded him, so he did. (Genesis 7:18-22)

God promises to start life all over again through Noah, his children, and the animals and food contained in the Ark. The purpose of the Flood was total destruction and judgment on a world gone mad with evil.

> They ate, they drank, they married wives, they were given in marriage, until the day that Noah entered the ark, and the flood came and destroyed them all. (Luke 17:27)

God was angry. He was determined to destroy the pristine environment that was created to assist man in the management of the planet and that had begun to deteriorate under the initial sentence of "death" delivered in the Garden. Although "thorns and thistles" had begun to resist the efforts to grow food, the flawless function of the initial design was still favored by a structure that was designed to last forever.

The myriad forms of life had been subjected first to the "rule" of man as the co-regent under the authority of the Creator. Centuries had passed since the death principle had been inserted into the creation, and "violence" had grown throughout the world to the point where God could only see "evil" in the thoughts of that which was under the "dominion" of man.

Lucifer and his minions had done their work well. Man and all that was associated with him had reached a point in their rebellion and in their evil thinking that embraced all living.

The Flood

More on this when the next volume of this study is published, but there can be no mistake that the sorrow of God brought the Judgment of God. "The world that then existed perished, being flooded with water" (2 Peter 3:6). The detailed description that follows in Genesis 6-8 leaves no doubt. The judgment of a holy and omnipotent God is an awful thing to be told about. Although none who went through that event are alive today, the careful description preserved was made by those eyewitnesses.

It is no accident that every culture from every age retains some record of such an event. How could it not be? Unique to everything humanity knows, the global Flood that God instituted is a terrifying reminder that the Creator is capable of utter destruction of that which He has made, when those whom He has made utterly rebel against the One who made them.

It is popular today to muse that God, if He really exists, could not or would not destroy that which He loves. The lie told by Lucifer to Eve still echoes in the empty hearts of mankind. Perhaps the main reason that many wish to ignore the evidence for God's judgment by water is that the annihilation of billions of men, women, and children in that sudden execution of holy verdict goes well beyond "our kind" of God.

"Religion" puts many faces on God. Holy books tell different stories about how to appease the God of their own making, but all such religious dogmas provide "steps" or "ways" to "reach" some sort of ultimate agreement, with a hope that everything turns out all right.

Nothing could be further from the truth.

God is loving and kind and merciful. All of His omniscience and His omnipotence have been directed to solving the eternal problem of sin. It is His expressed desire that "all should come to repentance" (2 Peter 3:9). The great Creator of all things in heaven and earth "will have all men to be saved, and to come unto the knowledge of the truth" (1 Timothy 2:4). However, when all has been done to bring repentance, when the "speech" and "knowledge" is declared day and night by the heavens (Psalm 19:1-4), and the "invisible things" of God's power and divine nature have been clearly displayed for all in every place and during all of time, those who reject and deny what they know to be true are "without excuse" (Romans 1:20).

> God is jealous, and the LORD avenges; The LORD avenges and is furious. The LORD will take vengeance on His adversaries, And He reserves wrath for His enemies; The LORD is slow to anger and great in power, And will not at all acquit the wicked. (Nahum 1:2-3)

> The LORD is good, A stronghold in the day of trouble; And He knows those who trust in Him. But with an overflowing flood He will make an utter end of its place, And darkness will pursue His enemies. (Nahum 1:7-8)

Only Six Chapters

There are only six chapters that log the events of the First Age. Six chapters covering a little more than 1,600 years. The rest of Scripture, the remainder of Genesis, 38 other books of the Old Testament and 29 books in the New Testament, all relate the sovereign care of a holy God bringing about the reconciliation of the Godhead to man, and the constant message of the "Good News."

Only six chapters, yet within their short pages are written the foundations of all that follows. Only six chapters, but the Creator draws us back time and again through the rest of Scripture, that because He is the Creator, you and I have every reason and hope of redemption. Only six chapters, but in them we can see reflected the awful end of sin let loose and the terrible impact of the lying and murderous heart of the Enemy, Lucifer. Only six chapters, nevertheless the clarity of Satan's strategy and the foolishness of Eve's deception are laid bare for all to see. Only six chapters, still rarely read and more rarely applied, in which the longsuffering of the Creator's heart aches for His image to return willfully to His love, but finally only "Noah found grace in His sight."

The First Age ends. God's longsuffering toward those who had everything placed in front of them is finished. The Flood of destruction buries the world in graves of mud and water. That age is over. Our age has begun.

> Now then, we are ambassadors for Christ, as though God were pleading through us: we implore you on Christ's behalf, be reconciled to God. (2 Corinthians 5:20)

ABOUT THE AUTHOR

 Dr. Henry Morris III holds four earned degrees, including a D.Min. from Luther Rice Seminary and the Presidents and Key Executives MBA from Pepperdine University. A former college professor, administrator, business executive, and senior pastor, Dr. Morris is an articulate and passionate speaker frequently invited to address church congregations, college assemblies, and national conferences. The eldest son of ICR's founder, Dr. Morris has served for many years in conference and writing ministry. His love for the Word of God and passion for Christian maturity, coupled with God's gift of teaching, has given Dr. Morris a broad and effective ministry over the years. He has authored numerous articles and seven books, including *The Big Three: Major Events that Changed History Forever* and *Exploring the Evidence for Creation*.

FOR MORE INFORMATION

Sign up for ICR's FREE publications!

Our monthly *Acts & Facts* magazine offers fascinating articles and current information on creation, evolution, and more. Our quarterly *Days of Praise* booklet provides daily devotionals—real biblical "meat"—to strengthen and encourage the Christian witness.

To subscribe, call 800.337.0375 or mail your address information to the address below. Or sign up online at www.icr.org.

Visit ICR online

ICR.org offers a wealth of resources and information on scientific creationism and biblical worldview issues.

- ✓ Read our daily news postings on today's hottest science topics
- ✓ Explore the Evidence for Creation
- ✓ Investigate our graduate and professional education programs
- ✓ Dive into our archive of 40 years of scientific articles
- ✓ Listen to current and past radio programs
- ✓ Watch our *That's a Fact* video show
- ✓ Visit our Science Essentials education blog
- ✓ And more!

Visit our Online Store at www.icr.org/store
for more great resources.

INSTITUTE
for CREATION
RESEARCH

P. O. Box 59029
Dallas, TX 75229
800.337.0375